THE
BOOK
OF
JOB

Other Books by E. W. Bullinger:

THE BOOK OF JOB

- *The Oldest Lesson in the World*

- *A New Translation*

E. W. *Bullinger*

KREGEL PUBLICATIONS
Grand Rapids, Michigan 49501

The Book of Job, by E. W. Bullinger. Published in 1990 by Kregel Publications, a division of Kregel, Inc. P. O. Box 2607, Grand Rapids, MI 49501. All rights reserved.

Cover Design: Don Ellens

Library of Congress Cataloging-in-Publication Data
   The Book of Job.

   Reprint. Originally published: Eyre & Spottiswoode.
   Includes a new translation of Job with explanatory and critical notes by the author.

      p.   cm.
   1. Bible. O.T. Job—Commentaries. I. Bible. O.T. Job. English. Bullinger, 1990. II. Title.

BS1415.B77   1990   223'.1077   90-36536
                                             CIP
   ISBN   0-8254-2291-4 (pbk.)
   ISBN   0-8254-2292-2 (dlxe. hbk.)

      2 3 4 5 6 Printing / Year 97 96 95 94 93

Printed in the United States of America

CONTENTS

PREFACE

FEW Books of the Bible have received more attention than the Book of Job ; both as to translations and as to commentaries. The Apocalypse, perhaps, exceeds it ; because of its relation to the future, in which we are naturally more interested.

The Book of Job carries us back to the remote past, and contains the oldest lesson in the world. It is significant that this oldest book should be devoted to imparting that knowledge, in comparison with which all other knowledge sinks into insignificance. It is the lesson which is essential to our having peace with God for Time, and to our enjoying the peace of God for Eternity.

In the first part of this work we have endeavoured to set this forth ; and in the Second Part we have given a new translation, concerning which a few words are necessary.

No apology is needed for adding one more to the many excellent presentations of the Book of Job : because there are six points which make this to differ from all previous translations ; and which, taken together, make the present effort quite distinctive in its character.

1. It is METRICAL. The decasyllabic measure has been chosen because the stateliness of that rhythm accords with the weighty language and lofty themes of the original, better than any other ; and certainly better than the jingle of the Anapæstic measure.

2. It is based on the literary STRUCTURE of the book. This, we believe, is, for the first time given in full ; in sum, and in detail. Over and above its own inherent beauty and interest, the

structure is most useful, if not necessary, because it gives the SCOPE of the various passages, and thus enables us to judge as to the sense in which certain difficult words and phrases are to be understood.

Thus the *Structure* determines the Scope ; and the *Scope*, in turn, furnishes the key to the interpretation of the words.

3. THE FIGURES OF SPEECH also are noted as far as possible. These again guide us as to the translation ; and their use is seen to be important as throwing light on many, otherwise enigmatical, expressions. It is the observance of Figures of Speech which has given Bengel's Commentary on the New Testament a unique place among such works. His example in such a matter is one which it is wise to follow, however humbly and imperfectly.

To translate a Figure of Speech *literally* is to obscure the very point for which it was used, to lose the emphasis it was intended to mark, and to miss the truth it was meant to teach.

4. Our aim also has been to make our Translation as IDIOMATIC as possible. Too close an adherence to the literal rendering of *words* necessarily leads to English which, to say the least, is often incoherent ; and conveys no definite sense to the English reader.

Literality, indeed, is required ; but it must be literality to the *sense* and not merely to the words. The English reader must have the same idea in his mind that was in the mind of the Foreign writer, irrespective of the actual words employed in conveying that meaning.

This, of course, applies to a translation from any language into English. The first requisite is that it must be English. This is a condition which must take precedence even of verbal faithfulness : because, unless we can understand the English, we cannot judge whether it represents the original faithfully or not.

We have therefore striven to translate the Hebrew *idioms* into the corresponding English *idioms*, rather than the Hebrew *words* into English *words*. In all such cases we have given the literal meaning of the Hebrew words in our notes, so that our readers may see exactly what has been done in order to obtain the sense ; and judge for himself how far that has been accomplished.

In this we have followed the example of the Translators of the Authorized Version. They give, for example, the beautiful English rendering of Gen. xxix. 1, "Then Jacob went on his journey," but they point out in the margin that the Hebrew idiom is "*And Jacob lift up his feet.*" So in Psalm xx. 3 they beautifully turn the Hebrew, thus, "The LORD . . . accept thy burnt sacrifice." But they explain in the margin that the Hebrew rendered "accept" means to "turn to ashes"; because that was the way in which the Lord accepted a Sacrifice. He *turned it to ashes*, by causing Divine fire to fall from the heavens and consume it. This is how He "had respect" to Abel's offering: this is how he "testified of Abel's gifts": this is how Abel "obtained witness that he was righteous" (Heb. xi. 4).

We have followed the example thus set in the A.V.: which is for this reason a "Version," while the R.V., being more literal to the *words*, is more correctly a "Translation," rather than a "Version."

Our aim has been, therefore, to translate into English *phrase*, and not merely into English words; to keep to the solemnity of the style of the Authorized Version, and not to vulgarize it by adopting twentieth-century English.

In the sacredness of its diction the A.V. has never been surpassed in any language. By its, sometimes, too strict adherence to Hebrew idioms, it has actually caused them to pass into, and become absolutely, English idioms.

We must not, however, confuse such idioms with English Archaisms; for the two are quite distinct: For example, "held his peace" is old English and not Hebrew; so are such expressions as "three score and ten," "give up the ghost," &c.

On the other hand, many pure Hebraisms have become naturalized English expressions, and are now the common property of both languages: *e.g.*, "at the hands of;" "by the hand of," "with the edge of the sword," "respecter of persons," "sick unto death," &c.

All this will show the difficulties which are inherent in any such attempt as the present ; and will give us a claim to the indulgence of our critics for any failure in attaining our high ideal.

.5. It is CRITICAL. We have followed the Hebrew Text of Dr. Ginsburg's magnificent and monumental work. His Critical Massoretic Text of the Hebrew Bible * must henceforth be the standard for all subsequent translations.

We have availed ourselves of his readings, and given his critical notes, in which he has recorded his own assured conclusions, as well as those based on the documentary authority of ancient Codices and Versions.

We have called attention to only a few of his more " conjectural" readings, where they seemed to be of importance.

6. THE DIVINE NAMES AND TITLES have all been indicated either in the Translation (where the Rhythm allowed it), or in the Notes. Those used in this book may be thus defined and distinguished.

ELOHIM is God, as the *Creator*, carrying out His *will*; God, standing in the relation of Creator to His creatures.

EL, is God, as the *Omnipotent*. The Creator showing forth His power in carrying out His *work*. " The Almighty " would have been, perhaps, the most appropriate rendering, had not this word been, in the A.V., appropriated as the rendering of " Shaddai."

ELOAH is the God who is to be *worshipped* and *reverenced*, the living God, in contrast with all idols and false gods.

ADONAI is God as *the Ruler* in the earth ; and this in relation to the whole Earth, rather than as limited to His own People. It is thus distinguished from Jehovah.

JEHOVAH is *the Eternal God,* " Who is, and was, and is to come." The self-existent God, Who stands in *Covenant* relation to His own People.

SHADDAI is God as *All-Bountiful*. The giver of every good gift ; the fountain of all Divine help ; and the supplier of all

---

* Published by the Trinitarian Bible Society of London, 1894.

human need. Not merely Almighty as regards His power, but All-Bountiful as regards His resources.

These are the Divine titles used in the book of Job, and it will be observed that *Eloah* and *Shaddai* are the titles that specially mark the character of the book.

In our judgment, all the Divine Names and Titles should have been preserved in their original forms in translating the Bible into any language. They should have been *transferred* (with explanations) instead of being *translated*. No one word in any language can ever explain all that is contained and implied in the Hebrew original.*

We have not ventured systematically on so bold a course ; but we have adopted it where possible in certain cases, especially with the names *Eloah* and *Shaddai*. When we have not been able to do this, we have indicated the different titles in the notes. We have also uniformly distinguished them by the use of different types : for example:—

ELOHIM, God the *Creator*, we have printed " God."

EL, God the *Omnipotent* or *Almighty*, we have printed " GOD."

ELOAH, God the object of *Worship*, we have printed " 𝕲𝕺𝕯."

ADONAI, God the *Ruler* in the Earth, we have printed " Lord " (as in A.V.).

JEHOVAH, God the *Eternal* One, we have printed LORD (as in A.V.).

SHADDAI, God as the *All-Bountiful*, we have printed " GOD."

Thus, the distinguishing features of the following version are :

1. That it is Rhythmical.
2. That it based on the Structure of the book.
3. That it notes the Figures of Speech.
4. That it is Idiomatic.
5. That it gives the critical readings of Dr. Ginsburg's Hebrew Bible.
6. That it distinguishes the various Divine Names and Titles.

---

* To adopt the *heathen* names and titles, and use them to represent the God of revelation is a still greater mistake.

These six points give our New Translation a special character. They fully justify our attempt; and they absolve us from all suspicion of presumption in aiming at the production of such a work. To combine them together in one book was worthy of our best efforts.

We do not suppose, for a moment, that what we have been able to do is superior to what others have done. But, if, in parts, we have accomplished what some have left undone, or succeeded where others have failed, it is due, not to our own merit, but to the great distinguishing principles on which the work is based; while any imperfections are due to our own failure in carrying them out.

We are conscious only of an honest endeavour to make the book itself, and its important lesson, more clear.

Nothing can add to our own pleasure in translating, and to the pleasure of those who shall read it, but the pleasure experienced in the heart by learning the great lesson which it teaches.

May we, together, come to the knowledge of Divine " Wisdom "; and, while we justify God and condemn ourselves, learn how mortal man can be just with God ; and that, while God is just, He is the Justifier of all who believe in the Lord Jesus.

Christ is the " spirit." In the book of Job we have the " body." But, " as the body without the spirit is dead," so the " letter " of the word without Christ (the " spirit ") is dead also. May His words be spirit and life, *i.e.*, true spiritual life, to ourselves.

E. W. BULLINGER.

PART 1

The Oldest Lesson in the World

or

"The End of the Lord"

as seen in the Book of Job

Ye have heard of the patience of Job
And have seen the end of the Lord;
That the Lord is very pitiful,
And of tender mercy.   —*James 5:11*

THE OLDEST LESSON IN THE WORLD

or

"THE END OF THE LORD" AS SEEN IN THE BOOK OF JOB

" Ye have heard of the patience of Job, and have seen the end of the Lord, that the Lord is very pitiful, and of tender mercy "
—(Jas. v. 11).

THE BOOK AND ITS STRUCTURE.

WE have all "heard of the patience of Job." But, the great and important question is this, Have we "seen the end" which the Lord had in view in all His dealings with Job? The "end" which He brought about in His own perfect way?

The object and purpose of the book are one. Whatever is said and done; whoever speaks or acts; all has reference to one person; and all is designed to bring about one "end."

It is a long book. It consists of forty-two chapters, relating to various events, and different agencies; all brought to bear upon one person, and all directed to one "end"—"the end of the Lord."

We see Heaven, and Earth, and Hell; Jehovah, and Satan; the Chaldeans, and Sabeans; fire from heaven, and wind from the wilderness; Job's friends, his wife, and children, all engaged and employed in order to secure one "end."

It is a wonderful book in itself, apart from either the patience of Job, or the end of the Lord.

We might study it with reference to the history involved in the book; its national character; its place in the Canon of Scripture; the time when it was written; the various references to arts and sciences, to natural history, to astronomy, to various objects of Nature, such as jewels, etc. We might study its eschatology; its knowledge of mineralogy, metallurgy and mining operations. We might notice its language; the words and expressions employed, especially those that are peculiar to the book. All these and many other matters might well form subjects of separate study : but we leave all these; because, however interesting each subject might be in itself, it is not the " end " for which the book is given to us.

Ancient it is beyond all dispute. It probably belongs to the period covered by the book of Genesis; and, possibly, to the time of Abraham.* Its lesson, therefore, is the oldest lesson we could have; and it takes us back to the first lesson taught in the Bible itself.

In Gen. i. and ii. we have the creation of man. In Gen. iii. we have the fall of man, and the chapter ends with the statement that man was driven out from the Garden of Eden in judgment (v. 24). Then, in Gen. iv., what have we but *the way back again* to God, in grace? God's way, which Abel took; and man's way, which Cain invented.

This, therefore, is the oldest lesson in the world. It is the first great lesson which stands on the fore-front of revelation; and the lesson of the book of Job follows this up and expands it by answering the solemn question, " How should man be just with God ? "

This is not only the oldest lesson, but it is the most important lesson that it is possible for us to learn. If we know not this lesson, it matters not what else we may know. Our knowledge may be vast, extensive, and deep on all other subjects; but it will not carry us beyond the grave.

But the knowledge of this lesson will serve us for eternity; and secure our eternal blessing and happiness. If we know this lesson, it matters little what else we do *not* know.

---

* See note on ch. i. 1, in New Translation.

No wonder then that this oldest lesson in the world is thus set at the very opening of God's Word, following immediately upon the record of the Fall. No wonder that, thus, at the threshold of the Word of God, we have the foundation of Gospel truth securely laid.

The "end" which the Lord had in view in the book of Job was to enforce this lesson in the most powerful way; a way which should serve as an object lesson for all time; and by the manner in which it is set forth should impress its importance upon the hearts and minds of all.

Its very structure is designed to attract our attention by exhibiting in a wonderful manner the perfect workmanship of the Spirit of God. The Structure itself speaks to us, if we have ears to hear. It says: If the outward form of the book be so perfect, how perfect must be its spiritual lesson; and how Divine must be its one great object; viz., "the end," which Jehovah had in view from the beginning; "the end" which was so blessedly accomplished; and "the end" for which it is given to us.

The Structure of the book is as follows:—

THE BOOK OF JOB AS A WHOLE.

A | i. 1-5. Introduction. Historical.

  B | i. 6—ii. 10. Satan's assault. Job stripped of all.

    C | ii. 11-13. The Three Friends. Their arrival.

      D | iii. 1—xxxi. 40. Job and his friends.

        E | xxxii.—xxxvii. Elihu.

      D | xxxviii. 1.—xlii. 6. Jehovah and Job.

    C | xlii. 7-9. The Three Friends. Their departure.

  B | xlii. 9, 10. Satan's defeat. Job blessed with double.

A | xlii. 11-17. Conclusion. Historical.

We will now consider these members in this order; and watch the process by which Jehovah brings about His own "end"; and accomplishes His own purposes.

The Law Of Believing

INTRODUCTION

A. (chap. i. 1-5.)

THE introduction is exceedingly simple. A few brief sentences tell us all that is necessary for us to know about Job:—

Where he lived (*v*. 1).
What he was (*v*. 1).
What he had (*v*. 2, 3).
What he did (*v*. 5).
What he said (*v*. 5).

He was perfect: Heb., םָּ (*tām*), *upright, sincere, without guile*. He did possess that wisdom and understanding which fears the Lord, and departs from evil; but the only true wisdom, which always *justifies God and condemns one's self*, he did not know.

True wisdom is to know what is "a broken heart" and "a contrite spirit." These are the sacrifices with which God is well pleased; and apart from these all other "wisdom" and all other sacrifices are worthless. *Rom̄s 8:1?*

Until man knows this he cannot know either God or himself.

To teach Job this important lesson is the "end" of all that we read in this book. All that is done and all that is said is intended to do for Job

What the "mighty famine" did for the lost son (Luke xv.);
What another famine did for Joseph's brethren (Gen. xliv. 16);
What Nathan's parable did for David (2 Sam. xii. 1-13);
What a glorious vision did for Isaiah (chap. vi. 1-5), and for Daniel (chap. x. 1-8);
What a wondrous miracle did for Peter (Luke v. 1-8).

The same work must be done for Job; and the same result must be produced in his case as in theirs.

As the lost son confessed " I have sinned " ;

As Joseph's brethren acknowledged " We are verily guilty " ;

As David said " I have sinned against the LORD " ;

As Isaiah confessed " I am undone . . . unclean " ;

And as Daniel declared " My comeliness was turned into corruption " ;

So must Job be brought to say, " I am vile " (chap. **xl**. 4).

" I abhor myself," " I repent in dust and ashes " (chap. xlii. 6).

This is " the end of the Lord," for the Lord Himself must be the teacher of this Divine lesson.

Man may be used by God to bring it about ; but God alone can be the bringer near of His own salvation, and the bestower of His own righteousness.

All this is quite apart from mere " religion," as such. Job was religious ; just as the heathen may be " very religious."[*] Religion is the attempt of man to become righteous by morality and ordinances ; but, the moment God produces a broken heart and a contrite spirit, the sinner is lifted completely out of the region of religion, and becomes the possessor of the " righteousness of God " Himself.

The book of Job, therefore, as we have said, is the illustration and the spiritual enlargement of the oldest lesson in the world as first taught in Gen. iv. 1-5. It is an object lesson which exhibits before our eyes the Divine answer to man's great question—the question of this book :

" How shall mortal man be just with God ? "

The first time the LORD God speaks to man after the Fall, He sets forth in his brief question, " Where art thou ? " the lost and helpless condition of man.

This is the first great lesson which man has to learn ; and his attempt to answer this great question is that which forms the first step in his attainment of true " wisdom."

[*] See Acts xvii. 22, R.V., margin.

6 *The Oldest Lesson in the World*

#1 The first question of the Bible is intended to reveal to man his lost condition ; and when he has discovered this, he asks the first question in the New Testament, intended to express this conviction, when he cries " Where is He ? " (Matt. ii. 2).   Where is the Saviour whom Thou hast provided for lost sinners ?   Where is the Saviour whom Thou has given and sent ?

The answer to this question is the oldest lesson in the world.

Unless we recognize this, as the " end " and design of the book, we shall never understand it, or learn its lesson for ourselves.

Jehovah dwells only " with him that is of a contrite and humble spirit " (Is. lvii. 15) ; to this man only, He says, " will I look " (Is. lxvi. 2).   But neither the one nor the other is seen in the case of Job, until we have come to the end of the book, and have " seen the end of the Lord."

The " end of the Lord " was not merely to teach Job what man was, or what the world was.

#3 The deceitfulness of man and the hollowness of the world are soon discovered by all.   It needs no special Divine process to learn that lesson.

The men who flattered him in his prosperity were the very ones to treat him with contumely in his adversity (see chaps. xxix.—xxx.).

Those who shouted " Hosanna to the Son of David," shouted " Crucify Him " a few days later.

When the lost son had plenty to spend, he had plenty to share it with him ; but when " he began to be in want, no man gave unto him " (Luke xv. 13, 16).

Sad it is to learn all this about the deceitfulness of man, if we have not previously learned the faithfulness of God.

True, we have " heard of the patience of Job " ; and if that had been all there was to hear, it would have been only an additional ground for his self-confidence ; and a ground for our own depression and disappointment ; for we fail to produce such patience as his.

But there is something for us to *see* as well as to *hear ;* and that is, " the end of the Lord " ; even that " the Lord is very pitiful and of tender mercy." But this is seen only by those who have themselves been made broken in heart, and contrite in spirit, under His mighty hand.

The one who ends this blessed work is the one who begins it. He began it here with this question to the Adversary in the first chapter; and he ends it with His double blessing in the last chapter.

THE ADVERSARY'S ASSAULT

B. (chap. i. 6—ii. 10.)

THE structure is as follows:—

B | F | **a** | i. 6. Presentation of the Adversary.
             b | i. 7. Jehovah's question.
                c | i. 8. His approbation of Job.
                    d | i. 9-11. Calumniation of the Adversary.
                        e | i. 12-. Limited permission given.
                            f | i. -12. Departure of Adversary.
                                g | i. 13 - 19. Inflictions (Job's possessions).
                                    h | i. 20, 21. Job's patience.
                                    i | i. 22. Job not sinning.

    F | **a** | ii. 1. Presentation of the Adversary.
             b | ii. 2. Jehovah's question.
                c | ii. 3. His approbation of Job.
                    d | ii. 4, 5. Calumniation of the Adversary.
                        e | ii. 6. Limited permission given.
                            f | ii. 7-. Departure of Adversary.
                                g | ii. -7. Infliction (Job's person).
                                    h | ii. 8-10-. Job's patience.
                                    i | ii. -10. Job not sinning.

We now come to witness the process by which this wondrous work was carried out; and to see the "end" which was thus brought about.

It is opened with the Adversary's assault on Job. An assault permitted by God, and used and over-ruled by Him, in order to accomplish His purpose. He can make the wrath of man to praise Him; and He can make the enmity of Satan to serve Him.

The Idiom of Permission

This assault of the Adversary is given us in chap. i. 6—ii. 10, and is divided into two parts; one part corresponding with the other, member for member.

The first part affects Job's *possessions*, and the second affects Job's *person*; and the whole member is presented in the form of an extended alternation.

Job was tempted to "curse God";* but, he did not thus sin. Instead of falling under this temptation, he uttered those memorable words, "The Lord gave and the Lord hath taken away; blessed be the name of the Lord" (chap. i. 21). When tempted a second time to "curse God,"* he replied, "Shall we receive good at the hand of the Lord, and shall we not receive evil?" (chap. ii. 10).

Beautiful as this is, it is only partly true; because it assumes that all our *evils* and *losses* are ruled by the Lord. It is true that He rules; but, He also over-rules. He rules our good, and over-rules our evil. Job's words manifest wonderful resignation, but it is only *religion*. Such sentiments can be expressed, and yet the speaker may not know either God or himself; and he may be wholly destitute of a broken heart and a contrite spirit.

All that Job here uttered, could be said without these inward evidences of Divine workmanship; and of true wisdom.

It is this workmanship which we are to *see* in this book. It is this which manifests "the end" which the Lord had in view for Job, and for us.

Divine Love ruled and over-ruled all. It wounded that it might heal: it brought low that it might lift up: it humbled that Job might be exalted, for ever and ever.

To bring about this end Satan was allowed to disturb

---

* In spite of the fact that the current Hebrew Text, here, has "bless God," both the A.V. and R.V. translate it "curse God," under some fancied, but mistaken, idea that the word can bear both meanings. The real explanation is that, though they are incorrect as translations, they are correct as to fact; for chaps. i. 5, 11, and ii. 5, 9, are among certain of the "emendations of the *Sopherim*," lists of which are carefully noted and preserved in the *Massorah*. See a further note on this in our New Translation, which follows in Part II.

Job's nest, and be the willing instrument which God would over-rule.

There is much that is mysterious in these first two chapters. They lift the veil for a brief moment and show how it is " against wicked spirits in heavenly places " that our conflict is waged.

There is nothing here for us to explain. It is written to explain unseen things to us. All is blessedly clear and simple to *faith*, where *reason* is useless.

Job's is not the only case which Scripture gives us as to the activities of the great Adversary.

The Twelve Apostles were allowed to be " sifted : " and the Lord prayed, not that Peter might not fall, but that Peter's faith might not fail. It was the failure of Peter himself that was the trial of his faith, and proved it to be more precious than gold that perisheth.

To this end, Infinite love controls and permits and over-rules all, and causes " all things to work together for good to them that love God, to them who are the called according to His purpose " (Rom. viii. 28).

This is why Satan was allowed access to our first parents. It was to bring forth the precious promise of the seed of the woman, and the announcement of Satan's doom (Gen. iii. 15).

This was why he was allowed to bruise the heel of the Lord of glory and of life ; not only that His people might be saved, but that " by death " he who had the power of death might be ultimately destroyed (Heb. ii. 14), and that his *head might be crushed* for ever.

This is why he is allowed to have a part in the destruction of " the flesh ; " it is that " the spirit may be saved in the day of the Lord Jesus " (1 Cor. v. 5).* Satan intends one thing, but God uses him for another; and works out the very opposite to Satan's will. The man who was thus " delivered " to Satan for the destruction of the flesh (1 Cor. v. 5) was afterwards restored and blessed (2 Cor. ii. 1-11), and Satan got no " advantage."

---

* See *Things to Come*, May, 1903, page 131.

This is why he was allowed to receive one who was "delivered" to him; it was that such an one thereby might learn "not to blaspheme" (1 Tim. i. 20).

This is why he is allowed to send his messengers as a thorn for the flesh, to buffet the saints of God; it is that they may thereby learn and prove the sufficiency of Divine grace, and the fulness of Divine power (2 Cor. xii. 7-9). Satan may intend one thing, but God uses him for another. In all these things he is a minister—used for the ultimate blessing, comfort and help of the people of God, and for their present spiritual profit.

He cannot go beyond the limits assigned to him. This is revealed in these chapters: see "e," and "*e*," chap. i. 13; ii. 6.

He was allowed to be the author of Job's trials and losses: but all his labour was wasted; for it ended in Job's receiving a double blessing for time, and for earth, and "the righteousness of God" for ever and ever.

May we have grace to learn the same precious lesson, and receive the same everlasting blessing.

May our eyes be opened to see the great lesson of this book, and the perfection of the Divine words and ways which brought about "the end of the Lord."

JOB AND HIS THREE FRIENDS

D. (chaps. iii. 1—xxxi. 40.)

WE may pass over the small member C (chap. ii. 11-13), the three verses which tell of the arrival of Job's three friends, Eliphaz, Bildad, and Zophar. That member is necessary to connect the threads of the history; but only a few words are used over the brief announcement of the fact.

We come, therefore, at once to the next member, "D." It is a large one, consisting of twenty-nine chapters. It contains and records the conference of Job with his three friends; the design of which is to show that man, apart from Divine revelation, has not true wisdom and cannot find out or know God: and cannot understand or know himself. Until man has this knowledge, he will neither justify God nor condemn himself. He may understand Jehovah's " works," but His " ways " cannot be known. His works are seen by all; but His ways are secret and hidden, and can be known only by revelation to His People. Hence we read (Ps. ciii. 7):

> " He made known his WAYS unto Moses,
> His ACTS unto the children of Israel."

It is this great truth which is now to be first shown us in this book. The first part of the lesson is *negative :* that man by searching cannot find out God ; or attain to true heavenly wisdom. This is the point of this member.

There are three series of these conferences, in which each takes part.

The following is the Structure : *

---

* For an explanation of these Structures see *A Key to the Psalms; The Vision of Isaiah,* and other works by the same author and publisher.

D. (iii. 1—xxxi. 40). *Job and his Friends.*

D | Z | iii. Job's Lamentation (Introduction).

G¹ | k¹ | iv., v. Eliphaz.
  l¹ | vi., vii. Job.
  k² | viii. Bildad.
  l² | ix., x. Job.
  k³ | xi. Zophar.
  l³ | xii.—xiv. Job.

G² | k⁴ | xv. Eliphaz.
  l⁴ | xvi., xvii. Job.
  k⁵ | xviii. Bildad.
  l⁵ | xix. Job.
  k⁶ | xx. Zophar.
  l⁶ | xxi. Job.

G³ | k⁷ | xxii. Eliphaz.
  l⁷ | xxiii., xxiv. Job.
  k⁸ | xxv. Bildad.
  l⁸ | xxvi.—xxvii. 10. Job.
  k⁹ | xxvii. 11—xxviii. 28. Zophar.*

Z | xxix.—xxxi. Job's Justification (Conclusion).

We do not propose to expand or to further elaborate the respective utterances of the various speakers.†

Too much importance may easily be placed upon them; for, after all, they are merely the gropings of the human mind to "find out God"; only the effusions of darkened understandings.

We must not quote the sentiments, either of Job or his friends, as though they were necessarily Bible-truth. We have the true, and truly inspired, record of what these men said: but it does not follow that what they said was necessarily either true or inspired.

---

* We attribute this member to Zophar. For our reasons, see note on chap. xxvii. 11 in New Translation.

† This will be done exhaustively in our New Translation, given in Part II.

No! Jehovah, when He speaks later in the book, distinctly declares that they had "darkened counsel by words without knowledge" (xxxviii. 2). They may have been aged men, and great; but, as Elihu says, "great men are not always wise, neither do the aged understand judgment" (chap. xxxii. 9).

At the "end" of the whole matter Jehovah tells the three friends that "ye have not spoken of me the thing that is right" (xlii. 7, 8). Neither had Job, until he confessed himself a sinner. THEN Jehovah could add, "as my servant Job hath." But that is not yet; at this stage they did not know God; and Job did not know himself.

It would therefore, as we have said, take us too far from the end we have in view to go into detailed examination of all their utterances.

We must content ourselves with noticing the drift or scope of these gropings of the human mind; and in doing this we shall see that man has not changed during the course of centuries. Their imaginations are the same with those of men to-day, their reasonings, too, are the same.

Eliphaz reasons on human experience.
Bildad reasons on human tradition; while
Zophar reasons on human merit.

If we look at the three colloquies as a whole, the one great lesson for ourselves is this: that man, with all his wisdom, and all his powers, cannot get to know God, and cannot meet man's needs. He can neither satisfy the righteous claims of God, nor heal the wounds of the sinner's heart.

All these reasonings were wrong in their conclusions, as they were false in their logic. They reasoned from the *particular* to the *general*: *i.e.*, they argued that what they had seen and observed in their own respective spheres was true universally.

They may speak truly of the "works" of God, and of what they had seen in the case of individuals; but it did not follow that they could gather from these few cases what was the law which regulated the "ways" and dealings of God with mankind.

Eliphaz is the first to answer Job's complaints.   His three utterances are given (1) chaps. iv., v., (2) chap. xv., and (3) chap. xxii.

His reasonings, as we have said, are based on human experience.   He argued from the particular to the general, and hence arrived at a wrong conclusion.   He based his argument on his own experience.   " As I have seen " is the burden of his speech. As he had " seen " that it was the wicked who always suffer, and the righteous who prosper, so he concluded that as Job was suffering he must therefore have committed some dreadful sin.   At first he only insinuates this.   He asks Job if he had not noticed the same thing himself.   He says (chap. iv. 7-9)* :

iv. 7. Bethink thee : when has the guiltless been destroy'd ?
         Or when where any upright ones cut off ?

    8. I've always seen, that they who evil plough,
        And mischief sow, they ever reap the same,

    9. They perish, smitten by the blast of **GOD** ;
        And by His angry blast they are consumed.

Again in chap. v. 3-5, Eliphaz says :—

v. 3. I—when I've seen the foolish striking root,
        Have forthwith shown what would take place ; [and
            said] :—

    4.   ' His children will be far from safety set,
           ' And crushed to death when passing in the gate,
           ' With no one near at hand to rescue them.

    5.   ' His harvest he will eat, still famishing,
           ' E'en though he take it from the hedge of thorns :
           ' A snare doth wait to swallow up their wealth."

---

* In all our quotations we give our own translation.   It will be literal to the *sense*, and to the Hebrew idiom, though it may not be always so to the words.   It will at any rate be *English* which can be understood.   It is by no means a paraphrase.   It may be taken as faithfully representing the original, and will often be found more literal even to the *words* than some other translations.   (See *Things to Come*, March, 1903, page 106.)

As we give, in Part II, the translation of the whole book by itself, we shall relegate all the *notes* to that, and not interrupt the flow of the words here.   Anything necessary to explain differences between our translation and that of others will be found in those notes.

So, in his second address, Eliphaz again appeals to experience (chap. xv. 17-21) :—

xv. 17. Give heed to me : and thee I will instruct ;
     And that which I have seen I will declare :

18. (Which wise men plainly have made known to us,
     And have not hid them : truths their fathers taught :

19. The men to whom alone their land was given,
     And among whom no alien passed). [They said] :—

20.   ' The wicked sorely labours all his days,
     ' His years reserved for the oppressor's greed,

21.   ' A voice of terror ever fills his ears :
     ' And when he prospers, then the spoiler comes.'

And so Eliphaz proceeds to the end of his second discourse, to show how, according to his experience, it is ever the wicked who suffer and are cut off, while the good are rewarded and preserved.

In his third address (chap. xxii.), Eliphaz enforces the same argument; and appeals to Job, begging him to mark well that it is ever thus with the wicked and the good. He says :—

xxii. 15. Oh, that thou would'st consider well the way
     Which wicked men of old have ever trod.

16. They, who were snatched away before their time ;
     Their strong foundation swept, as with a flood.

17. Who, unto GOD did say,
               ' Depart from us ' !
     [And ask'd] What Shaddai could do to them !

18. Yet, He it was who filled their homes with good.
     This way of wicked men is far from me.

19. The righteous see that THEY may well rejoice ;
     The innocent will laugh at them [and say] :—

20.   ' Surely OUR substance hath not been destroyed ;
     ' While THEIR abundance is consumed with fire.'

Job has not much difficulty in dealing with such arguments as these. After again bewailing his misery, he says (chap. vi. 22-27) :—

vi.   22. Came ye because I said, Give aught to me ?
           Or, Of your substance bring to me a gift ?
       23. Or, From the adversary's power deliver me ?
           Or, Ransom me from the oppressor's hand ?
       24. Teach me, I pray ; and I will hold my peace :
           And make me understand where I have erred.
       25. How forcible are words of uprightness !
           But as for YOUR words, how will THEY convince ?
       26. Do YE reprove by fast'ning on MY words,
           When one who's desperate speaks [at random] like
       27. The wind ?   Orphans ye might as well assail ;
           And feast upon the miseries of your friend.

BILDAD proceeds upon similar lines : except that he reasons
from the experience of many, rather than from his own (the
experience of one).   He goes back to antiquity, and leans on the
authority of the " Fathers."   He speaks, as Eliphaz had done, of
the merited end of those who forget God : implying that Job's
condition proved that his troubles were deserved.   He says (chap.
viii. 8-13) :—

viii.   8. Enquire, I pray thee, of the former age ;
           And of their fathers set thyself to learn.
        9. (For we're of yesterday, and nothing know :
           Yea, as a shadow are our days on earth).
       10. Shall THEY not wisdom teach, and to thee tell
           Wise things from their experience [such as these] :
       11.   ' The reed : Can it grow high without the mire ?
              ' The flag : Can it thrive where no water is ?
       12.   ' While yet 'tis green, and while it stands uncut,
              ' Sooner than any grass 'tis withered up.
       13.   ' So is the end of all who GOD forget :
              ' So perisheth the hope of godless men."

After elaborating this point, Bildad gives the other side of the
picture (chap. viii. 20) :—

viii. 20. But upright men GOD never casts away ;
           Nor will He take ill-doers by the hand.

To all this JOB has ready his reply (chap. ix. and x.). Bildad's words had no more weight than those of Eliphaz; for Job answers:—

> ix. 2. Most surely do I know that this is so:
>   But how can mortal man be just with GOD?
> 3. If man contend in argument with HIM,
>   Of thousand things he could not answer one.
> 4. However wise of heart, and stout of limb,
>   Who ever bravèd HIM, and prosperèd?

ZOPHAR next follows; and he repeats the same charges. But he does not appeal to experience, or to the past; he enforces the necessity of human merit more baldly than the other two. His teaching is exactly like that of the present day. He preaches the gospel of humanity. He talks of man "preparing his heart" and "putting away his sin," as the ground and means of securing God's favour: and that, without good works, there is no hope for man. Referring to Job's previous words, he says (chap. xi. 2-6, 13-15, 20):—

> xi. 2. Will not a mass of words admit reply?
>   And must a man of lips perforce be right?
> 3. Thy talk may put to silence mortal men:
>   THEM thou may'st mock, none putting thee to shame.
> 4. Thou mayèst say indeed to one of THEM,
>   'Pure is my doctrine: in His eyes I'm clean.'
> 5. But, oh! that Eloah would speak to thee:
>   HIS lips unclose; and, speaking, stop thy mouth,
> 6. And show thee some of wisdom's secret depths,
>   That they are far beyond all that is seen.
>   Then wouldst thou know that GOD exacteth less
>   Than all that thine iniquity deserves.
> xi. 13. [But as for thee]: Hadst thou prepared thy heart,
>   And stretched forth thy hands to Him in prayer,
> 14. If sin were in thine hand, 'twould be forgiv'n;
>   Evil had been removed from thy tent.

15. Thou wouldst thy face uplift without a stain ;
    Yea, thou wouldst stand secure, and need not fear :
16. For all thy misery thou wouldst then forget ;
    Or think of it as waters passed away.   . .

20. But as for wicked men, their eyes will fail,
    And every refuge to them useless prove.
    Their hope will vanish like a puff of breath.

Brave words are these ! but they are not the truth.   They show that the speaker (like his companions) knew neither God nor Job.

No one with any knowledge of God would speak of Him as exacting anything of a poor, helpless sinner as a ground of merit.

No one who knew anything of man could adjure him to prepare his heart ; for " the preparations of the heart are from the Lord " (Prov. xvi. 1).

Doubtless man *ought* to prepare his heart ; and, if he were right, he *would* do so.   If he were not a fallen creature he *could* do so.

But this is just the very central point of the whole question.

Man *is* fallen.   He " cannot turn and prepare himself, by his own natural strength and good works, to faith, and calling upon God."

What then is he to do ?   Ah ! that is the very thing that Job's friends cannot tell him.   They can talk of everything else ; but, when it comes to this, they stop short, or speak words that are utterly vain and useless.

" Natural Religion " is the burden of their theme.   Though proceeding on different lines, using different arguments, and appealing to different evidences, they were all agreed, as all false religions are to-day, in one thing ; and that is, that *man must do something* to merit God's favour.   If he does it, he will be rewarded.   If he does it not, he will be punished.   They cannot agree as to what that *something* is to be ; but they are agreed that it must be *something ;* and if your something is not like theirs, they may

---

* Article x. of *The Thirty-nine Articles of Religion.*   See John vi. 44, 65. Eph. ii. 8.

perhaps kill you ! as Cain killed Abel.   That is an important fact
in this oldest lesson in the world.   Hence, neither ELIPHAZ'S
experience, nor BILDAD'S tradition, nor ZOPHAR'S merit, could
bring relief to JOB.   As Jehovah declared (chap. xxxviii. 2), they
" darkened counsel by words without knowledge."

Yes, that was the secret cause of all their failure.   " Without
knowledge."   They said many things that were true and sublime;
eloquent and beautiful; but they knew not, and, therefore, could
not speak the truth of God.

Truth first wounds before it heals ; but they only hurt, and,
therefore, could not comfort.   They produced complaint, but not
conviction.

Job's answer to Zophar shows the effect of his argument.   He,
like the others, had condemned Job ; but he had not convinced
him.

Job replies (chapter xii. 2-4) :—

   xii. 2. Ye are the people : not a doubt of that :
        And as for wisdom, it will die with you.

      3. But I have intellect as well as you :
        And I am not inferior to you.
        Who hath not knowledge of such things as these?

      4. Sport to his friends ! And have I come to this !
        Ev'n I, who call on ⒼⓄⒹ, and whom He hears.
        A just, a perfect man, to be your sport.*

In chap. xiii. 1-5, Job again answers Zophar, and says :—

   xiii. 1. Behold, all these things mine own eye hath seen ;
        Mine ear hath heard, and understood them all.

      2. What ye know, I know also, even I.
        In no one thing do I fall short of you.

      3. It is to Shaddai that I would speak ;
        With GOD to reason, that is my desire.

      4. But as for YOU ; framers of lies are ye ;
        Physicians of no value are ye all.

---

* Perhaps in allusion to chap. xi. 12.

5. Would that ye altogether held your peace.
   That, of itself, would show that ye are wise.

Again in chap. xvi. 2-4, Job replies in the same strain to Eliphaz :—

xvi. 2. Of such like things I have abundance heard:
   [Yea], ministers of trouble are ye all.
3. Shall such vain words come never to an end?
   Or what emboldens thee to answer still?
4. For I also could speak as well as you.
   If YE were in distress instead of ME,
   I could heap words together against YOU ;
   Against you I could shake my head in scorn.

Again in chap. xix. 2-6, and 21, 22, Job answers Bildad, and says :—

xix. 2. How long will ye [thus grieve and] vex my soul?
   And break me all to pieces with your words?
3. Already, ten times, me ye have reproached,
   And yet are not ashamed to wrong me thus.
4. Be it that I have sinnèd as ye say :
   My sin is with myself [and God] alone.
5. If still 'gainst me ye magnify yourselves,
   And plead against me that I must have sinned ;
6. Then know that Eloah hath overthrown
   My cause ; and made His net to close me round.
xix. 21. Have pity ; pity me, O ye, my friends ;
   For 'tis Eloah's hand hath stricken me.
22. Why take on YOU that which pertains to GOD ?
   Will not my body's ills suffice for you ?

Zophar now makes his second address (chap. xx.) ; but it is the old theme : "the triumphing of the wicked is short " (*v.* 5). He ends it with the words :

xx. 29. Such is the sinner's portion sent from God.
   And such the lot GOD hath appointed him.

In his third address,* which, as we have seen from the structure above (page 13), is contained in chap. **xxvii. 11—xxviii. 28**, Zophar takes up and repeats the very words with which he had concluded his second address, **xx. 29.**

Zophar commences by saying that he also can teach, and that this he will do by showing what are God's ways and dealings with unwise men who do not fear Him or depart from evil; for His "hand," or power can be clearly seen.

xxvii. 11. I would now speak about the ways of GOD ;
    And Shaddai's dealings [with you] not conceal.

  12. Ye, surely, must have seen them for yourselves :
    Or, are ye then, so, altogether vain ?

  13. THIS is the lot of wicked men from GOD :
    Th' oppressor's heritage from Shaddai's hand :

  14. If children multiply, 'tis for the sword :
    Of bread, his offspring will not have enough :

  15. Their issue will be buried at their death,
    But widows will not lamentation make.

  16. Though silver, like the dust, he should heap up,
    And raiment make in number like the sand ;

  17. Though he prepare, the just will put it on ;
    His silver will the innocent divide.

  18. The house he builds : 'tis frail as is the moth's ;
    Or, as the hut which vineyard watcher makes.

  19. He lies down rich, [his wealth] not gathered in : †
    He openeth his eyes,—and it is gone !

  20. Terrors will overtake him as a flood :
    A whirlwind in the night will sweep him off.

  21. The East-wind catcheth him, and he is gone :
    Yea, as a storm, it hurls him from his place.

---

* For our reasons for assigning this portion to Zophar, see notes in our New Translation.

† See note in New Translation. His wealth is all put out in trade or at usury : he wakes up one morning to find it all lost.

22. He, who before, was wont to flee from him*
    Will now come down on him, and will not spare;
23. In triumph he will clap his hands at him;
    And hiss him forth from out his dwelling-place.

Thus Zophar sums up the one great argument which all the three friends had united in using against Job.

It is impossible for us to regard the above last quotation as the utterance of Job, inasmuch as Job's own arguments were exactly the opposite.

This will be clearly seen if we compare it with what were really Job's views as he expressed them in ch. xii. 6 and xxi. 7-12 :—

xii. 6. Prosp'rous and peaceful are the spoilers' tents;
      Security is theirs who GOD provoke;
      Abundance doth Eloah give to them.

And again :—

xxi. 7. Why [suffers God] ungodly men to live,
      And to grow old; yea, to wax strong in power?

  8. With them, their seed's established : yea, with them,
     Their offspring live, and grow before their eyes.

  9. Their houses are in peace : they know no fear.
     No scourge descends upon them from 𝕲𝕺𝕯'𝕾
     hand . . .

 11. Their little children skip about like lambs;
     Their elder children mingle in the dance.

 12. With timbrel and with harp they lift their voice;
     And merry make with cheerful sound of pipe.

When we compare this with Zophar's sentiments in chap. xxvii. 13, we ask, Could Job, who held such views as these, so totally different from all that his three friends had urged with such persistence and force; could he have possibly uttered the words of chap. xxvii. 13-23—especially in the face of Elihu's words in chap. xxxii. 12 ? "None of you convinced Job."

---

* See note in New Translation.

This seems to complete the evidence, which we give in our New Translation, for considering chap. **xxvii. 11—xxviii. 28, as** the third and last discourse of Zophar.

In chap. xxviii. Zophar concludes the whole argument maintained by himself and his friends.

He takes high ground. His point is that, seeing God's "hand" or way, is to punish those who do not fear Him, and to inflict His judgment on those who do not "depart from evil," wisdom may be thus defined in his concluding words (xxviii. 28):—

> Lo! Wisdom is to reverence the Lord :
> And Understanding is to flee from sin.

Job was in trouble, and oppressed with his calamities : but he urges that this could not be on account of his sins; for he *was* possessed of this "wisdom" and "understanding." He *did* "fear the Lord," and "depart from evil ;" and yet he suffered.

This is the point of the whole contention. It is, here, all summed up in the briefest possible compass.

It was a libel on Job, for Zophar thus to speak.

The wisdom of which he spoke is quite within the reach of the natural man. Thousands exhibit this wisdom every day. They find that it pays. It is good policy. But it is only "copy-book" morality : like "Honesty is the best policy;" of which it has been said that he who is honest only because it is good policy, might be dishonest if it were better policy.

Moreover, Job did possess this wisdom. He claimed it ; and the Lord vouched for it in chaps. i. 8, and ii. 3.

So far, therefore, as Zophar's definition of "wisdom" went, it failed to establish his case against Job. And Job (in chaps. xxix.-xxxi.) proceeds to demonstrate this.

All the arguments of chap. xxviii. are verily correct if used of *true* wisdom, "the wisdom that is from above" (Jas. iii. 17).

It is *not* correct if used of the human wisdom of the natural man.

To "reverence the Lord," and to "depart from sin" does not, in, or of, itself, constitute the wisdom that is "from above." It is only a *part* of it: and we may not put a *part* as though it were the whole.

The true or heavenly wisdom ever *justifies God, and condemns one's self.*

One may " reverence " the LORD, and yet not justify Him.

One may "depart from sin," and yet not condemn one's self; but rather, find in this very departure a ground for self-justification, instead of self-condemnation.

The great " end " of this whole book is to show that heavenly wisdom is evidenced by a broken heart and a contrite spirit.

There can be no true fear of God without the one; and no effective departure from evil without the other.

Zophar's wisdom is only a part of what true wisdom really is. For a "broken heart" cannot but fear the LORD ; and a "contrite spirit" cannot but depart from the evil it laments.

It is Elihu's great mission to show what that wisdom is which cometh down from above. And he does this in chap. xxxiii. 27, 28; and xxxiv. 31. It is, he says, when man takes his place as a sinner before the mighty God.

We see the same great lesson in Psalm li., where the Divine Teacher Himself teaches David to say :

> "I acknowledge my transgressions :
> And my sin is ever before me.
> Against thee, thee only have I sinned,
> And done this evil in thy sight :
> That THOU MIGHTEST BE JUSTIFIED when thou
>   speakest,
> And be clear when thou judgest" (*vv.* 3, 4).

This is what God requires in the sinner. This is the " wisdom " which He alone imparts. Hence David goes on to say in the sixth verse :—

> "Behold, thou desireth truth in the inward parts;
> And in the hidden part THOU SHALT MAKE ME TO
> KNOW WISDOM."

This wisdom we do not know by nature. We have to be "MADE" to know it (see Prov. xxx. 24, margin; and 2 Tim. iii. 15).

In chap. xxxviii. 36, Jehovah Himself tells Job the same thing: *viz.*, that it is He

"Who hath put WISDOM in the inward parts;
And UNDERSTANDING given to the heart."*

The Lord Jesus gave utterance to the same great truth in Matt. xi. 19, and Luke vii. 35, when He said

"WISDOM IS JUSTIFIED OF HER CHILDREN."

This enigmatical (and perhaps proverbial) saying means in this case, that, CHRIST, who is "the wisdom of God" (1 Cor. i. 24: compare Prov. viii. 22, 23; and iii. 19), is ever justified by those who are His, and learn of Him what He, their wisdom, is.

The context shows that his enemies condemned Him, while they justified themselves. They said that He was a glutton and a drunkard; and that John had a devil. They, therefore, showed by this that they could not be His children; for Wisdom's children ever justify Him, and condemn themselves.

Job had not *this* wisdom yet. Nor did his friends know anything whatever about it. When Job had learned it, THEN he "*said the thing that was right*" (but not before), for then he condemned himself and justified God (ch. xlii. 7). His friends had to learn it after that; and take the place of death-deserving sinners, by laying their hand on the head of their burnt-offering, and thus *owning* that they deserved its death.

But they had not learned this in chap. xxviii. 28. They all knew that it was wise and prudent to fear the Lord and depart from evil; because this was the way to escape from His judgments and merit His favour. This was their experience and their constant contention. This was their good policy. These were their " good works," on which they depended.

While Zophar, therefore, urged this sentiment about " wisdom,"

* Compare chap. xxxv. 11, and xxix. 17.

against Job, neither the one nor the other knew what heavenly wisdom was. But this is what they were to learn ; for this is the oldest lesson in the world ; and " the end of the Lord " was to " make them to know " it.

In Job's last reply to Zophar, he has to meet this special point. But he falls back upon his old position ; and he holds fast to his own righteousness (ch. xxvii. 6). He thus justifies himself and condemns God.

Job saw in Zophar's words the insinuation that he did not possess what Zophar described as " wisdom," or "understanding": seeing that Job's calamities showed that he had not " the fear of the Lord " ; and had not departed from evil.

Job therefore proceeds to show that this argument of Zophar's would not hold : inasmuch as his wonderful former prosperity was evidence which proved that he must have possessed this wisdom, and feared the Lord (chap. xxix.) ; and his innocency of life (chap. xxxi.) was proof that the sudden reversal of his position (chap. xxx.) could not have come upon him on account of his sins.

These are the points of Job's last words. His concluding address is very beautiful : but we cannot give it here. We must refer our readers to our New Translation, where they will find these three points of his argument fully set forth :—

> (1) His former prosperity (ch. xxix.).
> (2) Its sudden reversal (ch. xxx.).
> (3) His innocency of life (ch. xxxi.).

In the course of the first of these chapters it will be noted that (in ch. xxix.) Job refers to *himself* no less than *forty* times! while the references to Jehovah are no more than *five!* It is all self. Self-occupation overshadows all. In ch. xxix. it is the " I " of his prosperity ; in ch. xxx. it is the " I " of his troubles ; in ch. xxxi. it is the " I " of his self-righteousness. Self is justified and God is condemned. How changed is this, when we come to " the end." There we have the large " I " indeed ; but oh! what a different " I " it then is.   Then, it is the " I " of heavenly wisdom; the " I " which condemns himself and justifies God.

> " I—am vile " ;
>
> " I—abhor myself " ;
>
> " I—repent in dust and ashes."

But that blessed " end " is not yet, as these three chapters will soon make manifest.

THE MINISTRY OF ELIHU

E. (chaps. xxxii.—xxxvii.)

WE now come to the ministry of Elihu. Its importance is shown, as we have said, by the fact that it occupies the central position among all the subjects of the Book. This may be seen by reference to the structure of the Book as a whole.

Elihu's ministry occupies the central place, because it is necessary, in order to explain what goes before, and to prepare us for what is to follow. It is necessary, so that we may have it pointed out to us where Job and his three friends were all, alike, wrong. The root error of each side to this controversy is laid bare by Elihu; and the true remedy is plainly declared.

His ministry occupies no less than *six* chapters (chaps. xxxii.-xxxvii.); and this great central member has its own structure, as have all the others.

We must content ourselves with giving the general plan of it as a whole, without going into further minute detail. Neither is it necessary for us here to do more than select such portions as serve to bring out the one great subject of the book; and make manifest "the end of the Lord"—that "end" for which the book is written.

The ministry of Elihu, according to its structure, falls into four parts. After the introduction (chap. xxxii.), we have :—

(1) His words to Job (chap. xxxiii. 1-33).
(2) His words to Job's friends (chap. xxxiv. 2-37).
(3) His words to Job (chap. xxxv. 2-16).
(4) His words on God's behalf (chap. xxxvi. 2—xxxvii. 24).

The connecting history of Elihu (chap. xxxii. 1-5) is given in prose; and is strictly historical in its character, setting forth the facts which must be known in order that we may have a proper understanding of the whole.

The two counts of the great indictment are set forth with unmistakable clearness. Like the keynote in music, they furnish us with the true point from which we are to start, and to which we are to return; and which is to be kept in view throughout.

These two counts are expressed as being at once the cause of Elihu's righteous anger, and the ground of his intervention. They are stated with the utmost distinctness and conciseness in chap. xxxii. 2, 3.

"Against Job was his wrath kindled, because he justified himself rather than God.

"Also against his three friends was his wrath kindled, because they had found no answer [*for Job*], and had condemned God."*

Elihu proves this in chap. xxxiv. 5, and 10-12; and the context shows the ancient reading to be the true one; and most in harmony, both with the text and with the context.

For Elihu proceeds :—

(1) To show Job's friends that they had not answered him.

(2) To point out to Job his great and fundamental mistake in justifying himself.

(3) To justify God, and speak on his behalf.

All this worked together to secure "the end of the Lord."

Elihu's ministry has this one peculiarity, which makes it stand out in sharp contrast with other ministries, ancient and modern.

It is all for God!

It is all on God's side; not man's. It is necessarily, therefore, against Job, and against his friends (Isa. lv. 8). Though being wholly for God, it is really for man's own best interests; because it is the only way to peace, and rest, and blessing.

---

* This is another of the emendations of the Sopherim. The primitive Hebrew Text was "God;" and the Sopherim say, in their Massoretic note, that they changed it to "Job." This change was made from a mistaken notion of reverence, and to avoid what they looked upon as bordering on blasphemy. (See note on ch. i. 5, in our New Translation; and Ginsburg's *Introduction to the Hebrew Bible*, pp. 345-367. See especially p. 361.)

His name, "Elihu," means *my-God-is-He.* "Barachel"* means *whom-God-hath-blessed.* The meanings of these names are in harmony with the ministry which Elihu was called to exercise. He was, "in God's stead," to minister God's blessing.

In a few brief sentences, he sums up the whole situation, and condenses the whole twenty-nine chapters of the discussion.

At the outset, he brings God in as the One who is alone to be considered in so great a matter.

This at once puts an end to all the strife of words.

Elihu does not reason, as the three friends of Job had done. He used no arguments based on human experience, human tradition, or human merit: for in all this could be found no answer to Job's great question (ch. ix. 2) :—

"How should Mortal Man be Just with God?"

No! There was "no answer."

No matter how clear the premisses might be; no matter how clever the arguments; or how sound the reasonings; or how true the experience; or how meritorious the works; "there was no answer."

Oh! what weighty words are these. Job was "righteous in his own eyes" (chap. xxxii. 1). And God alone could give the needed spiritual eyesight.

Job could meet all the wisdom of man. He could find an answer to what his friends brought forward. But all of them together could not answer Job's great question :

"How should Mortal Man be Just with God?"

Having explained his reason for intervening, and why he had delayed doing so till then; he at once lays bare the point at issue (chap. xxxii. 11-14). Elihu first addresses the three friends, and says :—

---

* Barachel was, it says, a "Buzite;" *i.e.,* he was descended from Buz, second son of Nahor, the brother of Abram (see Gen. xxii. 20, 21). Elihu would, therefore, appear to have been a family connection of Abram. (See longer note in New Translation.)

xxxii. 11. Lo ! I have listened unto your discourse ;
　　　　　To all your reas'nings I have given ear,
　　　　　Waiting till ye had searched out what to say.
　　　12. But, though to you I carefully gave heed,
　　　　　There was not one of you convincèd Job.
　　　　　Not one who really answered what he said.
　　　13. I pray you, say not ' We have wisdom found ' ;
　　　　　For God alone can put him right ; not man.

This exactly states the case. They had condemned Job, but
had not convinced him. This has ever been man's method from
that day to this. But God's way is first to *cónvince* a man, so
that man may then *condemn himself*. Unless, and until, that be
done, nothing is done. Truly, God's thoughts are not our
thoughts, nor our ways His ways (Isa. lv. 8).

Ah ! God alone knows how to do this. He can break the
hardest heart, and subdue the stoutest will. This is utterly
beyond man's power ; and altogether out of man's sphere. This
is the " end of the Lord," which is to be brought about before
the book closes.

Having put his finger on this, the weak spot in all that Job's
friends had said, he proceeds to do the same in the case of Job
himself. But, he first shows how well he is qualified to do this :

xxxiii. 1. And now, O Job, I pray thee hear me speak,
　　　　　And be attentive to my every word.
　　　　2. Behold, now, I have openèd my mouth ;
　　　　　My tongue shall utt'rance give, distinct and clear ;
　　　　3. For all that I shall say comes from my heart,
　　　　　My lips shall speak what is sincere and true.
　　　　4. God's Spirit made me [at the first] and [still]
　　　　　'Tis the Almighty's breath must quicken me.
　　　　5. If thou art able, answer me, I pray :
　　　　　Array thy words in order ; take thy stand.
　　　　6. Lo ! I am here—thou wished it—in God's stead.*
　　　　　And of the clay I have been formed [like thee].

---

* See chaps. xiii. 3, 18-22 ; xvi. 21 ; xxiii. 3-9 ; xxx. 20 ; xxxi. 35.

7. Behold, my terror will not make thee fear;
   Nor heavy will my hand upon thee press.

8. But surely thou hast spoken in mine ears,
   And I have heard a voice of words [like these]:

9.   'A man without transgression—pure am I:
   'Yea, I am clean; without iniquity.

10.   '[God] is against me; seeking grounds of strife;
   'And He doth count me as His enemy.

11.   'My feet He setteth fast within the stocks,
   'And taketh observation of my ways.'

12. Behold, thou art not just: I answer thee,
   HOW GREAT IS GOD COMPARED WITH
   MORTAL MAN.

13. Why, then, against Him didst thou dare complain
   That by no word of His He answereth thee?

14. For GOD DOTH speak. He speaks in sundry ways:
   Again, again, though man regard it not.

15. He speaks in dreams, and visions of the night.
   When, deep in slumber, lying on their bed,
   There falls on men an overwhelming sleep.

16. Then opens He their ear that they may hear,
   Pressing, as with a seal, the warning given,

17. To make a man withdraw himself from sin;
   Or keep him from the [dangerous] way of pride.

18. Back from the pit 'tis thus He keeps a man;
   And saves his life from falling by the sword.

19. He speaks again, when, chastened, on his bed,
   Another lies, his bones all racked with pain;

20. So that his daily food he doth abhor,
   And turns against his choicest dainty meat.

21. His flesh, it wastes away, and is not seen:
   His bones, before concealed, show through his skin.

22. Unto destruction he is drawing nigh;
   And death's dark angel waits to end his life.

23. Then, then He speaks with him by messenger,
    Who can interpret : One, 'mong thousands chief,
    Who will reveal to man HIS righteousness.
24. Then He doth show him grace [Divine, and
         saith],
      'Deliver him from going down to death ;
      ' A Ransom I have found—Redemption's price.'
25. Young, as a child, becomes his flesh again,
    And to his youthful days he doth return.
26. He supplication makes to Eloah,
    Who grace and favour sheweth unto him ;
    So that he looks unto [God's] face with joy.
    Thus He doth give to man HIS righteousness.
27. This, then, becomes the burden of his song :
      ' I sinned ! and I perverted what was right ;
      ' Although no profit from it did I gain.
28.   ' My soul HE hath redeemèd from the pit :
      ' My life shall yet again behold the light.'
29. Thus doth GOD speak in all these sundry ways :
    Time after time ; and yet again He speaks :
30. That from destruction He may save a soul.
    And make him joy in light—the light of life.
31. Mark this, O Job ; and hearken unto me,
    I will now speak : and, as for thee, hold thou
    Thy peace ; while I, with words of wisdom, teach.
32. If there be any answer, answer me.
    Speak : for I long to see thee justified.
33. If not, do thou then hearken unto me ;
    Hold thou thy peace, while wisdom I impart."

In answer to Job's complaint that God would not speak or
answer him, Elihu thus shows that God *does* speak to men in
various ways.　He speaks by His providence; in visions ; by
sickness ; and, above all, by His special messengers, whom He
sends to interpret Himself to men.　Just as the chief Messenger

Himself was sent, in later days, to "interpret* the Father"
(John i. 18).

In his further addresses, Elihu disposes of many other of the
false notions both of Job and of his friends.

Truth soon exposes folly. Job had said he was "pure," and
"clean," and "innocent" (ch. xxxiii. 9); while, in the very same
breath, he brings utterly false charges against God.

In one sentence Elihu lays the sharp axe of truth at this corrupt root, when he says, "God is greater than man." How
simple, and yet how powerful! Because it follows, of course,
that, if this be so, God must be the judge as to what is right and
wrong, and not man. He alone can determine the standard of
righteousness which He demands.

But this declaration which is thus placed at the foundation of
all that Elihu has to say, is the very truth that man will not have,
either then or now.

Whether he be religious or infidel; whether he speak from
platform or pulpit, man constantly sits in judgment on God; on
His works, on His Word, on His ways. Man presumes and dares
to decide what God has done; what God will, and ought to, do;
and what God has said. He gives high-sounding names to these
things, which only manifest his folly. He calls them "Science,"
and "Philosophy," and "Higher Criticism." He assumes the
position of Judge, and decides what is, or is not, worthy of God.
But in all this there is nothing new. It is exactly what God has
given us in this book of Job. Here we are shown that, what is,
has ever been. Job and his friends utter the same follies as those
we hear on all sides to-day. But

"GOD IS GREATER THAN MAN."

This is the great fact which puts everything in its right place.

When the time comes for Jehovah Himself to speak to Job,
this is the text He takes; this is the truth He enforces; and this

---

* This is the meaning of the Greek ἐξηγέομαι (*exegeomai*), from which we
have the noun *exegesis.*

it is, with which Elihu commences, that brings about "the end of the Lord."

We cannot go through Elihu's ministry word by word, but we must notice two other passages (chap. xxxiv. 31-37 and xxxv. 2-16), in which he vindicates God, and speaks on God's behalf.

xxxiv. 31. If Job had spoken unto GOD, and said :
'I have borne chastisement : and never more
32. 'Will I transgress.   That which I do not see
'Teach me Thyself.   If in the past I wrought
'Iniquity, I will not work it more : '
33. Shall He requite on thine own terms [and say]
'As thou wilt choose [so be it], not as I ' ?
Say therefore, now, O Job, if thou dost know.
34. For ME, would men of understanding speak :
Yea, every wise man listening now [will say],
35. 'Job, without knowledge, spoke in ignorance,
'And without understanding were his words.
36. Oh would that Job were proved unto the end ;
For his replies are those of evil men.
37. Rebellion he doth add unto his sin.
'Mong us, he, in defiance, claps his hands,
And against GOD he multiplies his words."

This is Elihu's estimate of Job, and of all who do not bow to the fundamental truth that "God is greater than man." In Job's case, Elihu's desire was granted ; for Job was tried and proved "unto the end"—"the end of the Lord."

In the next chapter, he again enforces the great truth (xxxv. 2-16), and continues his address.   He asks :—

xxxv. 2. Dost thou count this sound judgment ?   Thou didst say,
'My righteousness surpasses that of GOD ' ;
3. Yea, thou dost ask : What is the gain to thee ?
And, 'Shall I profit more than by my sin ? '
4. I—even I will make reply to thee,
And, with thee, to these friends of thine, as well :—

   5. Look up unto the heav'ns ; consider them :
      Survey the skies, so high above thy head.
   6. If thou hast sinned, What doest thou to Him ?
      Be thy sins many, What dost thou to Him ?
   7. If thou art just, What dost thou give to Him ?
      Or from thy hand what [gift] will He receive ?
   8. Thy sin may hurt a mortal like thyself :
      Thy righteousness may profit one like thee.

   9. Men make an outcry when they are oppressed ;
      They cry for help when 'neath the tyrant's pow'r ;
  10. But no one saith, " Where is my Maker—**GOD** ? "
      Who giveth songs to us in sorrow's night ;
  11. And teacheth us beyond the beasts of earth,
      And makes us wiser than the fowl of heaven.
  12. But, why He answers not, though men may cry :
      Is the o'erweening pride of evil doers.
  13. For vanity, GOD will in no wise hear,*
      Nor will th' Almighty hold it in regard.
  14. How much less, thee, when THOU dost say to HIM !
      ' I see Him not : [He doth not hear my cry'].

      Yet, judgment is before Him.   Therefore, wait.

  15. But now, because He hath not punishèd
      [Thou say'st] ' His anger doth not visit sin,
      ' Nor strictly mark widespread iniquity."
  16. Thus, Job hath filled his mouth with vanity,
      And, without knowledge, multiplied his words.

Having thus spoken to Job and his friends, Elihu goes on to speak on God's behalf (chapter. xxxvi. 2-5) :—

xxxvi. 2. Bear with me while I, briefly, make thee see
      That there are words to say on **GOD'S** behalf.
   3. My knowledge I shall gather from afar ;
      And, to my Maker, righteousness ascribe.

---

* See chap. xxx. 20 ; xxxi. 35 ; xix. 7 ; ix. 16, and compare xii. 4 ; xxiv. 1 ; Ps. xxii. 7, 8 ; xlii. 10, etc.

    4. Truly, no falsehood shall be in my word,
       Th' Omniscient One it is who deals with thee.
    5. Lo—GOD IS GREAT—but naught doth He **disdain** ;
       In power great, in wisdom great is He.

Elihu then goes on to expand this truth, fetching his knowledge from afar, as he had said; and thus he prepares the way for the ministry of Jehovah Himself.

THE MINISTRY OF JEHOVAH HIMSELF

D. (chap. xxxviii. 1—xlii. **6**.)

THE next great portion of this book is taken up with the Ministry of Jehovah Himself to Job.

This is the most important of all ; and it is the most beautiful.

It is important, because we have Jehovah acting as His own minister. He Himself becomes the preacher.

Surely, it is a matter of the intensest interest to ask in wonder, *What is the theme on which He will speak ?* what is the text which He will expound? For in this we shall discover what is to be, and ought to be, the great subject of all preaching and ministry to-day.

Whatever it was, it produced the desired effect ; and brought about, at once, "the end" which the Lord had in view from the beginning. It ended in bringing Job to occupy the only place where God brings near His righteousness.

What then was the text? and what the theme that produced this wondrous result ?

Elihu's ministry was designed to furnish both. It was thus absolutely necessary in order that it might prepare the way, by announcing the subject which Jehovah was so powerfully and abundantly about to enlarge, expound, and apply :

"GOD IS GREATER THAN MAN."

This was the theme that led up to the only answer that could be given to the great question of the book.*

"HOW SHOULD MORTAL MAN BE JUST WITH GOD?"

Elihu's declaration furnishes the key to and answers Job's question.

---

* See chaps. iv. 17 ; ix. 2 ; xv. 14; **xxxiv.** 5 ; and xxxiii. **9 above.**

May Jehovah use it for the eternal blessing not only of Job, but of all who devoutly study this book.

Let us note, and mark it well ; *Jehovah's address is entirely about Himself !* No other subject is allowed to share or distract our attention.

This it is that brings about " the end of the Lord. ' This it is that accomplishes the mighty work.

Oh ! what an important lesson for all who would minister or speak for God. He Himself is to be the one great theme of all our testimony. Nothing lower ; nothing less ; nothing different.

And what a blow to the new idea of "Evolution," whether Scientific or "Christian." Here, we have Jehovah in every line for four long chapters speaking of His own works as being each His own specific creation, and the result of his own creative acts.

Just as, in Genesis i., we have the great Creator speaking, moving, creating, making, and blessing, *thirty-five* times in that one chapter ; so here, in every line, Jehovah speaks of Himself as the Creator of everything in all its wondrous details as to object, and purpose, and effect. So that it is impossible to receive the testimony of the Word of God, and the conjectures of Evolution. There is not room for both. One must go.

If we accept God's Word, we cannot admit the very first idea of even what is called " Christian " Evolution. If we accept Evolution, then we make the Word of God worse than a lie ; we make it an imposture of the gravest kind.

According to Genesis i., and these four chapters of Job, God created each thing with its own specific attributes, and powers of reproducing "after its kind " ; each with its own definite object and purpose.

According to " Christian " Evolution, God did nothing of the kind. He created a "cell" : and from this, we are asked to believe, all else was *evolved !*

We answer, it is easier to *believe* God than to believe this hypothesis. To do the latter is simply *credulity*, and not *faith* at all : for no one has ever yet seen one thing evolve into a *different* thing. We can see flowers and animals "improved" or otherwise by cultivation ; but no flower has ever evolved into an *animal !* These can be respectively developed or improved, but if they be left, they at once revert to their original type, and do not go on to evolve into a higher and different species altogether.

No ; the two systems are *incompatible*. And we believe God. We accept the great truth here announced : that "God is greater than man." He is the Almighty Creator : and our testimony is to be of Him, and of His Word, and of His grace, and of His power, and of all His other wondrous attributes.

But, alas, to-day the pulpits are occupied with the praise of man ; man's wonderful discoveries and inventions are dwelt upon. His wisdom and cleverness are extolled. Man is practically deified ; while God is deposed, or bowed out of His own creation. It is the gospel of humanity that is preached, rather than the Gospel of God.

His Word, instead of being proclaimed, is criticised. And, instead of obeying it, man is sitting in judgment upon it !

This oldest lesson in the world, therefore, comes like a lightning flash, exposing the vanity of modern ministry, and illuminating the darkness by which we are surrounded.

No wonder "the end of man" is so different from "the end of the Lord." No wonder that, instead of the sinner's being humbled in the dust before the mighty God, he is exalted with self-righteousness and pride. No wonder that, instead of being brought down, he is puffed up. No wonder that the results of man's ministry are so opposite to the results of Jehovah's ministry, as we see it in this book.

The object and aim of the one is to make man moral and right for time ; while the "end" of the other is the humbling of man, so that he may be made Divinely righteous for ever.

The moral improvement of man is the end and aim of man to-day ; while the conviction of sin, as the condition of eternal blessing, is the object of Jehovah—"the end of the Lord."

The very precepts and persuasions addressed to men (whether

sinners or saints) only serve to minister to the natural pride of the human heart; and thus tend to defeat the very end in view.

They only lift man into a temporary sense of being more or less right; while the one object of the Gospel is to convict him of being altogether wrong: for this is the one necessary condition before man can know God's righteousness. Man must be humbled before he can be exalted.

Eliphaz, Bildad, and Zophar are as busy to-day as ever—trying to *make men good,* by reasoning and persuasion. But they only "darken counsel by words without knowledge."

Oh, for more, like Elihu, who shall speak "on God's behalf": who shall expose the vanity of this gospel of humanity; and point men to the living God.

This is the lesson which we learn from the fact that Jehovah, when He intervenes, and undertakes to accomplish all, where all others have failed, speaks only of Himself.

Apart from all that He says; apart from the beauty and glory of all that He reveals; the fact that Himself is His one great theme speaks to us, if we have ears to hear; and that fact says:— *True ministry is to interpret* (chap. xxxiii. 23) *the God of Grace to lost sinners.* And this was the object of Christ's own ministry on earth (John i. 18).

With this in our minds we shall be able better to understand and appreciate the address itself. It is divided into two parts: and at the end of each, Job manifests its Divine effect. At the end of the first half Job speaks, but only to say that he cannot say anything. And at the end of the last half, he speaks to some effect, and manifests "the end of the Lord."

The structure of Jehovah's address, as a whole, and in all its parts, is wonderful indeed. But we must refer our readers to our New Translation, where it is given in sum and in detail:

From that structure it will be seen that it is divided into two great parts, each of which is followed by Job's answer in a few brief lines: the first time to confess that he could say nothing; and then to confess that he had come to the end of himself, the end of his own righteousness, having at length reached "the end of the Lord."

Both parts of the Address of Jehovah are constructed on the same model.

The first consists of three appeals to Job, separated by two discourses about Himself: the former about His wisdom exhibited in its activities (in the Inanimate Creation); the latter about His wisdom manifested "in the inward parts" (in the Animate Creation).

The Second Address consists of three appeals to His power, separated by two brief consequences: the former a consequent Admission, the latter a consequent Inference.

The effect of the first address of Jehovah is to bring forth this first sign of conviction from Job's heart.

The very man who had said he was "a just and perfect man," that he was "pure" and "clean" and "without iniquity," now calls out,

"I AM VILE."

What has wrought this great effect? Only the ministry of Jehovah.

But His work is not yet complete.

He who had begun this good work will finish it (Phil. i. 6). And hence He goes on to continue and complete it.

Jehovah concludes His first address by asking Job :—

xl. 2. As caviller with [mighty] Shaddai,
   Contender with Eloah : Answer that!
3. And Job answered Jehovah, and said
   4. Lo! I am vile! What shall I answer Thee ?
   Rather, I lay mine hand upon my mouth.
   5. Already, I have spoken far too much ;
   I cannot answer. I will add no more.

Jehovah's second address is contained in chaps. xl. 6—xli. 34.

We must give enough of it to bring out the Divine skill which manifests "the end of the Lord."

xl. 6. Then Jehovah again addressed Job out of the **storm, and** said :—

Appeal to His Power : (General).

7. Now, like a strong man gird up thee thy loins :
  'Tis I who ask thee : make thou Me to know.
8. Wilt thou MY righteousness quite disannul ?
  And ME condemn ; that THOU may righteous seem ?
9. Hast thou an arm, then, like the mighty GOD ?
  Or, Canst thou thunder with a voice like His ?
10. Deck thyself now with glory and with might ;
  Array thyself with majesty and pow'r :
11. Send far and wide thy overflowing wrath ;
  And on each proud one look, and bring him **low.**
12. Each proud one single out, and humble him,
  Yea, crush the evil-doers where they stand.
13. Hide them away together in the dust ;
  Their persons in the deepest dungeon bind.

Consequent Admission.

14. THEN ALSO I MYSELF WILL OWN TO THEE
  THAT THY RIGHT HAND TO SAVE THEE
  WILL SUFFICE.

Jehovah ends the second part of his address with describing **Lev**iathan :—

Appeal to His Power: (Particular).

xli. 1. Canst thou draw up Leviathan with hook ?
  Or, catch as with [an angler's] line his tongue ?
2. Canst thou insert into his nose, a reed ?
  Or, Canst thou pierce his jaw through with a thorn ?
3. Will he make many humble pray'rs to thee ?
  Or, Will he ever say soft things to thee ?

4. Will he engage in covenant with thee
   That thou shouldst take him for thy life-long slave?
5. Wilt thou, as with some linnet, play with him?
   Or, Wilt thou cage him for thy maidens' sport?
6. Will trading dealers haggle o'er his price?
   And retail him among the merchantmen?
7. Wilt thou with darts attempt to fill his skin?
   Or, [fill] his head with spears for catching fish?
8. Lay thou thy hand upon him; though but once;
   Think only of the contest.   Do no more.
9. Behold, all hope of taking him is vain;
   Ev'n at the sight of him one is cast down.
10. None so foolhardy as to stir him up.

Consequent Inference.

BEFORE ME, THEN, [HIS MAKER], WHO CAN
  STAND?
11. WHO E'ER FIRST GAVE TO ME, THAT I SHOULD
  HIM
  REPAY? SINCE ALL BENEATH THE HEAV'NS
  IS MINE?

Jehovah then proceeds to speak in further detail of Leviathan;
and concludes as follows (chap. xli. 27):—

27. Iron he counts no better than a straw;
   And brass, no better is than rotten wood.
28. The arrow will not make him flee away;
   Sling-stones are only stubble unto him.
29. Like harmless chaff he counts the pond'rous club;
   And at the whizzing of a spear will laugh . . .
33. His equal is not found on all the earth;
   He hath been made insensible of fear.
34. On all things high he looketh [dauntlessly],
   And over all proud beasts himself is king.

This is followed immediately by "the end of the Lord," as
manifested in Job's answer (chap. xlii. 2-6).

Job's Answer.

2. I know, I know, that THOU canst all things do.
No purposes of THINE can be withstood.

3. [Thou asked'st—chap. xxxviii. 2] :—
    ' Who is this that counsel hides,
        And darkens all, because of knowledge void ? '
    'Tis I !—I uttered things I could not know ;
    Things far too wonderful, and past my ken.

4. But hear, I pray Thee, let me speak this once.
    [Thou said'st—chap. xxxviii. 3 and xl. 7] :—
            ' Tis I who ask thee : Answer me.'

5. I'd heard of Thee with hearing of the ear,
    But now that I have had a sight of Thee.

6. Wherefore I loathe myself; and I repent
    In dust and ashes.

Here then we reach the culminating point of this wonderful
book.

Jehovah's ministry had accomplished Jehovah's " end."

Job, now, justified God and condemned himself, and thus manifested his possession of true " wisdom."

Job was humbled in the dust, with ashes on his head : and
realized that in the light of God's glory and greatness, he was
nothing.

Ah ! we may try to be nothing ; and we may sing, " Oh, to be
nothing "; but all our trying and all our singing will never
produce that result; or bring us into this, the only place of blessing.

If we succeeded in our trying, it would be only artificial ; and
that can never take the place of what is real.   If we could thus,
by our own effort, bring ourselves to *feel* that we are nothing, *that*
would only be, in itself, a ground for feeling that we were something, after all.   If we were able, of ourselves, to bring about so
wonderful a result, it would only tend to increase our " confidence
in the flesh."

No ! If we would have the reality, and *be* nothing, as well as *feel* nothing, it must be brought about in the only way that can *really* accomplish it.   It must be Divinely produced if it is to be a Divine reality.

We must have a true sense of the glory and greatness of God. That alone will show us, and convince us, that we *are* " nothing." We shall soon *feel* it *then*.

A man may feel great and important while he stands in his own little garden ; but let him stand beneath the stupendous heights of snow-capped peaks ; let him be in the mighty ocean when its waves run mountains-high ; and then he will see himself to be the puny pygmy that he really is : then only will he realize his own impotence, and thankfully cast himself on God's omnipotence.

Oh ! what a crisis it is in a man's experience when he is brought to this point; to see and confess that he has been all wrong : having wrong thoughts of God, wrong thoughts of God's ways, and of God's words : with wrong thoughts about himself and about others.

Oh ! to get true thoughts of God.   This is to get right, indeed : and, if we be right here we shall be right about other things.

This is what we see as the result of Jehovah's own ministry. This is the " end of the Lord " with Job.   It was to produce this confession :

> " I am vile."
> " I abhor myself."
> " I repent in dust and ashes."

Here is the " I," indeed, but in a very different connection from that of chaps. xxix.—xxxi.

No more contention with God or man.

No more self-justification.

All such things lost in a true apprehension of the greatness and the glory of the living God.

This is far more than assenting to the doctrine of " moral depravity."

It is far more than saying we are "miserable sinners."

It is the experimental realization of the accomplishment of a Divine work :

> "Mine eye seeth THEE,
> Wherefore I abhor MYSELF."

These two things are inseparably linked together.   It is impossible to do the one without the other.

May it be the blessed portion and the happy experience of all who read these words.

CONCLUSION

C., B., & A. (chap. xlii. 7-17.)

WE must consider the remaining members together, as they all three form part of the moral conclusion; though the literary conclusion is confined to a few verses (11-17).

Now that "the end of the Lord" has been "seen," all else is, by comparison, a matter of very small importance.

It is necessary, however, that we should be told of the departure of Job's three friends, inasmuch as we were told of their arrival : that we should hear of Job's double blessing, as we heard of his double series of calamities.

All this is needful in order to complete the whole, and put the finishing touch to the book ; but a very few verses suffice to dismiss such details as these.

Nevertheless, they are worthy of our closest attention.

When Job got right with God, and had his new thoughts of Him ; he not only had new thoughts about himself, but about his friends, and all else.   In verse 10, we are told that

"HE PRAYED FOR HIS FRIENDS."

Yes, for those with whom he had so bitterly contended ; and toward whom he had used such opprobrious expressions : "He prayed for his friends."

He had called them "miserable comforters" ; and now, he was to be a blessed comforter to them.

He had called them "physicians of no value" ; and now, he would be a good physician, to their value for ever and ever.

Job was a new man ; and fervent prayers took the place of bitter words.

This is "the end of the Lord." It is perfect: for it is Divine.

His friends needed an "Interpreter" now: for they were not yet right with God. They had spoken "folly" about God, as He tells them, here (in verse 8). They had not spoken of God the thing that was right. Neither had Job, before he received the ministry of Jehovah. But, since then, he had.

For now he had said :—

> "I know that Thou canst do everything.   .   .   .
>
> "I am vile.   .   .   .
>
> "I abhor myself.   .   .   .
>
> "I repent in dust and ashes."

This was "the thing that was right"; and Job had said it. Twice over this is affirmed (verses 7 and 8). His friends had not yet said it, and thus had not yet come to that place of blessing. Therefore it was that they were commanded to offer a burnt offering ; and, that Job should pray for them.

How blessed for us to see the perfection of this Divine workmanship.

All Eliphaz's *experience* was gone.   All Bildad's *tradition* was flung to the winds.   All Zophar's *merit* was now seen to be of no avail.

All alike are now humbled before God.   All contention is over. The revelation of the glory of God, followed by the manifestation of His grace, has ended in conviction of sin, tears of repentance, the sweet savour of the burnt-offering, and the voice of prayer.

What more is there for us to be told ?   This:

The overthrow of the Adversary.   At the beginning, he despoiled Job of all his possessions : at "the end" "the LORD gave Job twice as much as he had before" (*v.* 10); and we are told "the LORD blessed the latter end of Job more than his beginning '
(*v.* 12).

This is "the end."   It was not Job's wisdom, or Job's good works : it was not Job's merit, or Job's repentance; but

"**The Lord gave**" (*v.* 10).

and

"**The Lord blessed**" (*v.* 12).

This explains the verse with which we commenced (James v. 11) : " Ye have heard of the patience of Job, and have seen the end of the Lord."

Job had been brought to the end of himself ; and was thus in a right position to see the " end of the Lord " : that, though He is very " great," yet He is also " very pitiful, and of tender mercy."

PART 2

A New Translation of The Book of Job

A rhythmical translation with the
structure in sum and detail, and
brief explanatory and critical notes.

A NEW TRANSLATION OF THE BOOK OF JOB

THE STRUCTURE OF THE BOOK AS A WHOLE.

A | i. 1-5. Introduction. Historical.

   B | i. 6—ii. 10. Satan's assault. Job stripped of all.

      C | ii. 11-13. The Three Friends. Their arrival.

         D | iii. —xxxi. Job and his friends.

            E | xxxii.—xxxvii. Elihu.

         D | xxxviii. 1.—xlii. 6. Jehovah and Job.

      C | xlii. 7-9. The Three Friends. Their departure.

   B | xlii. 10-13. Satan's defeat. **Job blessed with double.**

A | xlii. 14-17. Conclusion of his family history.

THE INTRODUCTION. HISTORICAL.

A. chap. i. 1-5.

A | A | i. 1. Job's character.

         B | 2. His sons and daughters. Their **number.**

           C | 3-. His possessions ;—great.

           C | -3. His position ;—great.

        B | 4. His sons and daughters. Their **unanimity.**

     A | **5.** Job's conduct.

A (page 54) chap. i. 1-5. *The Introduction. Historical.*

A | i. 1. There was in the land of Uz[1] a man whose name was Job.[2] This man was pure and upright, one who reverenced God,[3] and shunned evil.[4]

B | 2. And there were born to him seven sons and three daughters.

C | 3-. And his substance consisted of 7,000 sheep, and 3,000 camels, and 500 yoke of oxen, and 500 she-asses, and a very great household.

C | -3. Thus, this man was the greatest,[5] above all the other children of the East.

B | 4. Now, his sons were wont to hold[6] a feast, each one at his own house[7] and on his own day ; and they sent invitations[8] to their three sisters to eat and drink with them.

A | 5. And so it was, when these festival days came round, that Job sent [for] and purified his children [9]; and rising early in the morning, he offered up burnt offerings, according to the number of them all: for Job used to say [10]: 'It may that my sons have sinned ; and have cursed God[11] in their hearts.' Thus was Job wont to do continually.

---

[1] *Uz* עוּץ is probably the son of Nahor, Abram's brother. Gen. xxii. 21.

[2] JOB .אִיּוֹב means *the assailed*. He dwelt in Uz, and had for his friends three descendants of Esau, viz., Eliphaz, Bildad, and Zophar.

ELIPHAZ, of Teman in Idumea, was the son of Esau, and had a son called Teman, from whom the country took its name (Gen. xxxvi. 10, 11). Teman (named after Esau's grandson) was noted for *wise men* (Jer. xlix. 7); and is mentioned with Edom (Amos i. 11, 12). Compare Jer. xxv. 23, where both are con-

nected with Buz, the brother of Uz (Gen. xxii. 21).

BILDAD the Shuite. Shuah was the sixth son of Abraham by Keturah (Gen. xxv. 2). Dedan, the son of Bildad's brother, Jokshan (Gen. xxv. 3), is mentioned in connection with Esau, Edom, and Teman (Jer. xlix. 8).

Of ZOPHAR the Naamathite nothing is known. There was a town called Naamah on the border of Edom (Josh. xv. 41).

(For Elihu see note on ch. xxxii. 1).

Job was, probably, the son of Issachar (Gen. xlvi. 13), and went

down into Egypt. When Joseph
died, and the Israelites fell into dis-
favour, he, not unnaturally, removed
to Uz. There would be no reason
for his departure while Joseph lived.
In Uz he dwelt among the descendants of Esau, three of whom became
his friends. He was, however, not to
escape tribulation; but, instead of in
Egypt it came in Uz. There he
worshipped Abraham's God and
followed Abraham's religion. He
died out of Egypt. His first sons
being killed, his genealogy would
not be continued or reckoned.

Absolute evidence is impossible :
but no better evidence is forthcom-
ing for a different view.

[3] Heb. *Elohim.*

[4] He had therefore the wisdom
spoken of in ch. xxviii. 28, but not
the Divine wisdom which is from
above, which ever justifies God and
condemns one's self.

[5] Job is thus distinguished from
the people of the East among whom
he dwelt, " East " being used of
the country of Uz, which was east
of the writer and of Egypt.

[6] Heb., *went and made.*

[7] Heb., *each one on his day : i.e.,* his
birthday.

[8] Heb., *sent and called.*

[9] Heb., *them.*

[10] The verb must be taken in a
frequentative sense, as it was what
he said with regard to each festival.

[11] In these four passages, ch. i. 5,
11 ; ii. 5, 9 ; as well as in Psalm x. 3
and 1 Kings xxi. 10, 13, the
current Hebrew text has בָּרַךְ
(*barach*), *to bless.* But the A.V.
renders the passages in Job " curse,"
while in Ps. x. 3, and 1 Kings xxi.
10, 13, it renders it " bless," though
the Hebrew text is the same. The
commentators, by laboured arguments, strive in vain to show how
the one word can have both meanings. If this could possibly be
shown, it would be the most curious

phenomenon ever met with in any
language. As well might black be
made to mean white also, and
bitter to mean sweet.

The fact is that the translators
(at any rate, of the A.V.) do not
seem to have been acquainted with
the Massorah.

The Massorah consists of the
notes written in the margins of
all standard Hebrew manuscripts.*

These notes are not comments,
and do not contain anything by
way of interpretation. They relate
only to the words and letters of
the MS.

Their one design is to secure the
correct transmission of the Hebrew
text, so that not a word or a letter
may be misplaced, omitted, or
inserted.

Reduced fac-simile of MS. in the
possession of the Earl of Leicester. (Ex.
xxix. 36—xxx. 11.)

We give a fac-simile of a page of
an ancient MS., now the property
of the Earl of Leicester. It was

* See *The Massorah,* by the same
author and publisher, price one shill-
ing ; and Ginsburg's *Introduction to
the Hebrew Bible,* pp. 345- 367.

written about A.D. 1250-1300, and, as will be seen, it contains three columns of the text on the page, with two lines of Massorah at the top of the page, and five lines at the bottom, sometimes extending to nine lines.

Our illustration is a photographic reproduction of a page of the original MS. It is reduced in size, but it is sufficient to illustrate what we are endeavouring to explain.

Among the vast number of Massoretic notes written in the smaller writing above and below the text, is one that states as a matter of fact that several words in the primitive Hebrew text were deliberately altered or changed by its ancient custodians (called the Sopherim) from a mistaken idea of reverence for God.

Lists of these alterations are preserved in the Massorah. They are called "The eighteen emendations of the Sopherim." There are four separate and independent lists, apart from the Massorah; beside other passages noted in the Massorah, but not included in any list.

Among them are the seven passages mentioned above, where the word ‎לֵל‎ (*chalal*) *to curse*, stood originally in the primitive text ; but, out of a dislike to utter with the lips such an expression as " curse God," they put in its stead ‎בָּרַךְ‎ (*bārach*) *to bless*, relegating the original word ‎לֵל‎ (*chālal*) *to curse*, to the Massoretic notes ; and placed on record the fact of their

alteration, thus protecting the original primitive text, and preserving it for ever from being lost or forgotten. We profit to-day by the care thus exercised, and so are able to restore the primitive word.

Strange to say, that, with the word ‎בָּרַךְ‎ (*bārach*) *to bless*, in the current *Textus Receptus*, in all these seven passages, the A.V. has rendered it " curse " in Job. i. 5, 11 ; ii. 5, 9, and "bless" in Psalm x. 3, and 1 Kings xxi. 10, 13.* They have done this without giving any intimation of it to the general reader ; and without any information as to the Massoretic note.

The fact is it ought to be rendered " curse " in all the seven passages, in accordance with the primitive Hebrew Text ; and the alteration, made and noted by the Sopherim, should be ignored ; or relegated to the margin, with a note.

Psalm x. 3 should be rendered—

" The wicked boasteth of his heart's desire ;
And the covetous curseth, yea, abhorreth the LORD."

The renderings and marginal alternatives of both the A.V. and R.V. are sufficient evidence as to the perplexity of the translators in the absence of the only information that makes the passage clear.

---

* The R.V. has translated it "renounce" in the four passages in Job, with a note "Or, *blasphemed*"; while in 1 Kings xxi. 10, 13, it has "*curse*" in the text, and "*renounce*" in the margin; and in Psalm x. 3 it has "*renounce*" in the text, and "*bless*" in the margin!

THE ADVERSARY'S ASSAULT

B. (page 54) chap. i. 6—ii. 10.

B | F |a | i. 6. Presentation of the Adversary.

     b | i. 7. Jehovah's question.

       c | i. 8. His approbation of Job.

         d | i. 9-11. Calumniation of the Adversary.

           e | i. 12-. Limited permission given.

             f | i. -12. Departure of Adversary.

               g | i. 13-19. Inflictions (Job's possessions).

                 h | i. 20, 21. Job's patience.

                   i | i. 22. Job not sinning.

F |a | ii. 1. Presentation of the Adversary.

     b | ii. 2. Jehovah's question.

       c | ii. 3. His approbation of Job.

         d | ii. 4, 5. Calumniation of the Adversary.

           e | ii. 6. Limited permission given.

             f | ii. 7-. Departure of Adversary.

               g | ii. -7. Infliction (Job's person).

                 h | ii. 8-10-. Job's patience.

                   i | ii. -10. Job not sinning.

a | **i. 6.** Now it came to pass on **the day when** the angels[1] came **to present** themselves before Jehovah, that Satan also came among them.

b | 7. And Jehovah said to Satan, 'Whence comest thou ?' **And Satan** answered Jehovah, and said : **'From going** to and fro in the earth, 'and walking up and down therein.'[2]

c | 8. And Jehovah said to Satan, 'Hast thou considered[3] My servant 'Job ? Surely there is none like him on the earth, pure and up-'right, reverencing God,[4] and shunning evil.'

d | 9-11. And Satan answered Jehovah and said, 'Doth Job 'reverence God,[4] for naught ? Hast not Thou Thyself made 'a hedge about him, and about his house, and about all 'that he hath, on every side ? The work of his hands Thou hast 'blessed ; and his substance is increased[5] in the land. But put 'forth now Thy hand, and smite[6] all that he hath, and see 'whether he will not curse[7] Thee to Thy face.'

e | 12-. And Jehovah said to Satan, 'Lo ! all that he hath is [put] 'into thy power[8] : only against his person put not forth thy 'power.'[8]

f | -12. So Satan went forth from the presence of Jehovah.

g | 13-19. Now it was the day that his sons and daughters were eating and drinking wine in the house of their brother, the first-born, and there came a messenger to Job, and said: 'The oxen were ploughing, and the asses feeding beside 'them, when the Sabeans[9] fell upon them and took them. 'Yea, they have slain the servants with the edge of the 'sword ; and I only am escaped alone to tell thee.' While this one was still speaking, another came in, and said: 'A 'great fire[10] fell from the heavens, and burned up the 'flocks and the servants and consumed them ; and I only 'am escaped alone to tell thee.' While this one was yet speaking, there came another and said : 'The Chaldeans 'formed into three bands, and made a raid upon[11] the 'camels and took them. The servants also they have slain 'with the edge of the sword ; and I only am escaped alone 'to tell thee.' While he was speaking, another came in, and said : 'Thy sons and thy daughters were eating, and 'drinking wine in the house of their brother, the first-born, 'when, lo ! a great wind came from the desert, and smote 'the four corners of the house, and it fell upon the young 'people, and they died ; and I only am escaped, alone, to 'tell thee.'

h | 20, 21. Then Job arose, and rent his garment, and shaved his head, and fell to the Earth, and worshipped; and said:
'I came forth naked from my mother's womb,
'And naked [to the earth] shall I return.
'Jehovah gave ; Jehovah takes away.
'[Then] let Jehovah's name be ever blessed.'

i | 22. In all this Job sinned not, nor did he attribute folly to God.

a | ii. 1. Again it came to pass on the day when the angels [12] came in to present themselves before Jehovah that Satan also came in their midst to present himself before Jehovah.

b | 2. And Jehovah said to Satan, 'Whence comest thou?' And Satan answered Jehovah and said, 'From going to and fro in the earth and 'from walking up and down therein.'

c | 3. And Jehovah said to Satan, 'Hast thou considered [13] my 'servant Job; that there is none like him in the earth, pure and 'upright; one who reverenceth God [14] and shunneth evil; and he 'still holdeth fast his integrity, although thou didst incite Me 'against him, to destroy [15] him without cause?'

d | 4, 5. Then Satan answered Jehovah, and said:—'A skin [is 'exchanged] for a skin.[16] But all that a man hath will he give 'for his life. Put forth now Thy hand, and smite [17] his bone, 'and his flesh, and he will curse [18] Thee to Thy face.'

e | 6. And Jehovah said to Satan: 'Lo! he is in thy power,[19] 'only spare his life!'

f | 7-. Then Satan went forth from the presence of Jehovah,

g | -7. And smote Job with grievous sores [20] from the sole of of his foot to his crown. And he took him a potsherd to to scrape himself therewith, as he sat among the ashes.

h | 8-10-. Then said his wife unto him,[21] 'Dost thou still 'hold fast thine integrity? Curse [18] God [22] and die.' And he said to her:—

'Thou speakest as the foolish women speak.
'Shall we accept our blessings [as] from God,[23]
'And shall we not accept misfortune [too]?'

i | -10. In all this Job sinned not with his lips.

---

[1] Heb., בְּנֵי הָאֱלֹהִים (*benai ha-Elohim*) *sons of God*, is (in the Old Testament) always used of Angels: in this book (ch. xxxviii. 7), and in Gen. vi. 2. Ps. xxix. 1; lxxxix. 6. Dan. iii. 25. It is clear, therefore, that Job i. 6; ii. 1, and Gen. vi. 2, 4, are no exception to the rule. That some of them fell, we know from 2 Pet. ii. 4, and Jude 6, 7. The latter passage identifies the nature of that fall recorded in Gen. vi. 2, 4. It is for this that they are called in the emphatic Greek (1 Pet. iii. 19) "in-prison spirits," reserved for future judgment. In English idiom we should say *imprisoned spirits*.

[2] The Sept. reads "from wandering about under the heavens I have come." See Ginsburg's Hebrew Text and note.

[3] Heb., *set thine heart upon.*

[4] Heb., *Elohim.*

[5] Heb., *hath spread abroad.*

[6] Heb., *touch.* The idiom for injury, arising from the figure *Tapeinosis.*

[7] See note on ch. i. 5.

[8] Heb., *hand :* put by *Metonymy* for *power.*

[9] Heb., *Sheba,* put by *Metonymy* (of the subject) for a host of the people of Sheba.

[10] Heb., *the fire of Elohim.* By the Figure *Antimereia,* a Divine name is put for what is great, high, glorious, strong, or beautiful. So here *a great* fire. Compare Gen. xxiii. 6 ; xxx. 8. Ex. ix. 28. 2 Ch. xx. 29 ; xxviii. 13. Job. iv. 9. Ps. xxxvi. 6 ; lxviii. 15 ; lxxx. 10 ; civ. 16. Song viii. 6. Jer. ii. 31, &c. See *Figures of Speech,* by the same author and publisher, pp. 502, 503.

[11] Heb., *spread themselves ;* or, as we should say, *deployed.*

[12] See note on ch. i. 6.

[13] See note on ch. i. 8.

[14] Heb., *Elohim.*

[15] Heb., *swallow him up.*

[16] A "skin for a skin" was evidently a proverb, quoted by Satan, as expressing the usual principle governing human exchanges. But what will not a man give in exchange for his life ? (Compare Ps. xlix. 7, 8. Matt. xvi. 26.)

[17] See note on ch. i. 11.

[18] See note on ch. i. 5.

[19] See note on ch. i. 12.

[20] Heb., *sore.*

[21] The Septuagint here reads as the words of Job's wife : " How long wilt thou hold out, and say

' Behold, I wait yet a little while,
' Expecting the hope of my deliverance ? '

For, behold, thy memorial is cut off from the earth—[even thy] sons and thy daughters, the pangs and pains of my womb, which I bore in vain, with sorrows ; and thou thyself sittest down to spend the nights in the open air among the corruption of worms, and I am a wanderer, and a servant from place to place, and house to house, waiting for the setting of the sun, that I may rest from my labours and my pains, which now beset me. Now curse God and die."

[22] Heb., *Elohim.*

THE THREE FRIENDS: THEIR ARRIVAL

C. (page 54) chap. ii. 11-13.

C | A | a | ii. 11-. Their visit. *Hearing* of Job's calamities.
    | | b | -11. The reason.
    | B | 12-. Their sorrow. (Mental.)
    | *B* | -12. Their sorrow. (Symbolical.)
    | *A* | *a* | 13-. Their visit. *Seeing* Job's calamities.
    | | *b* | -13. The reason.

The Three Friends. Their arrival. **chap. ii. 11-13.**

A | a | **11-.** When Job's three friends heard of all his calamity which had come upon him, they came, each one from his own place : Eliphaz the Temanite, Bildad the Shuite, and Zophar the Naamathite.
   | b | **-11.** For they made an appointment to come to show sympathy with him and to comfort him.

        B | **12-.** And when they lifted up their eyes afar off, and, [at first], did not know him, they lifted up their voice and wept,

      B | **-12.** And rent, each one, his garment, and sprinkled dust upon their heads toward the heavens,

A | *a* | **13-.** And they sat down with him upon the ground, seven days and seven nights; and none spoke a word to him,
   | *b* | **-13.** For they saw that his grief was exceedingly great.

JOB AND HIS FRIENDS

D. (page 54) chaps. iii. 1—xxxi. 40.

D | Z | iii. Job's Lamentation. Introduction.

G¹ | k¹ | iv., v. Eliphaz's first address.
l¹ | vi., vii. Job's reply to Eliphaz.
k² | viii. Bildad's first address.
l² | ix., x. Job's reply to Bildad.
k³ | xi. Zophar's first address.
l³ | xii.—xiv. Job's reply to Zophar.

G² | k⁴ | xv. Eliphaz's second address.
l⁴ | xvi., xvii. Job's reply to Eliphaz.
k⁵ | xviii. Bildad's second address.
l⁵ | xix. Job's reply to Bildad.
k⁶ | xx. Zophar's second address.
l⁶ | xxi. Job's reply to Zophar.

G³ | k⁷ | xxii. Eliphaz's third address.
l⁷ | xxiii., xxiv. Job's reply to Eliphaz.
k⁸ | xxv. Bildad's third address.
l⁸ | xxvi., 1—xxvii. 10. Job's reply to Bildad.
k⁹ | xxvii. 11—xxviii. 28. Zophar's third address.

Z | xxix.—xxxi. Job's self-justification. Conclusion.

---

[1] For our reasons, assigning this member to Zophar, see the note on ch. xxvii. 11.

JOB'S LAMENTATION.

Z. (page 63) chap. iii.

Z | H¹ | iii. 1-9.   Birth lamented.

   I¹ | 10.   Reasons.

H² | 11-12.   Infancy lamented.

   I² | 13-19.   Reasons.

H³ | 20-23.   Manhood lamented.

   I³ | 24-26.   Reasons.

H¹. (above) **1-9.** *Birth Lamented.*

iii. 1. After this JOB opened his mouth, and cursed his day ¹

2. And JOB began ² and said :—

3. Perish the day when I was to be born,
Or night which said a man-child is brought forth.

4. That day ! may it be darkness evermore ;
Let not Eloah care for it³ above,
And let not light shed on it one clear ray.

5. Let darkness and the death-shade take it back ; ⁴
Let densest clouds upon it settle down ;
Let gathering darkness fill it with alarm.⁵

6. That night !   Let darkness take it for its own ;
Let it rejoice not, 'mid the other days,⁶
Nor come into the number of the months.

---

¹ Perhaps "his fate," as in xxx. 25, or the day of his birth.

² The Hebrew idiom "answered and said" must be rendered according to the context "asked and said," "prayed and said," whatever may be the nature of what is said. Here it means "began and said." Later on it means "concluded and said." A similar usage is found in the New Testament.

³ Compare Deut. xi. 12.

⁴ Compare Gen. i. 2.

⁵ As if denoting an impending storm.

⁶ Heb., *days of the year.*

7. Lo ! let the night be cheerless [1] evermore ;
   And let no joyful sound be heard therein.
8. Let those engaged in cursing days [2] curse this ;
   Those skilled to rouse the Dragon of the Sky.[3]
9. Let all the twilight stars thereof be dark.
   Let it look forth for light, and look in vain ;
   And may it nevermore behold the dawn.[4]

I[1]. (page 64) chap. iii. 10.   *Reason.*

10. Because it shut not up my mother's womb, [6]
    And so hid all this misery from mine eyes.

H[2]. (page 64) chap. iii. 11-12.   *Infancy Lamented.*

11. Why should I not have dièd in the womb ? [5]
    Or when brought forth, why not have then expired ?
12. Wherefore were [nursing] knees [7] prepared for me ?
    Or why were breasts [prepared] that I should suck ?

I [2]. (page 64) chap. iii. 13-19.   *Reasons.*

13. For then, in silence had I been laid down,
    I should have fall'n asleep and been at rest
14. With kings and councillors of Earth ;
    (The men who build their mouldering [8] monuments),
15. With princes who [in life] possessed much gold
    (And who, with silver, had their houses filled);

---

[1] Heb., *barren, i.e.,* barren of joy. Hence, *joyless, cheerless,* as in xv. 34 ; and xxx. 3.

[2] *i.e.,* sorcerers, who claim to make days unfortunate *(dies infausti).*

[3] *i.e.,* Leviathan or Egyptian Typhon, who by swallowing the sun-god produces eclipses. Job merely concedes this tradition for the sake of argument, without going any further into the matter. A similar reference may be seen in chap. xxvi. 13, and Isa. xxvii. 1.

[4] Heb., *the eyelids of the morn.*

[5] Heb., *the doors of my womb: i.e.,* in which I lay.

[6] So the Septuagint and Vulgate.

[7] *i.e., the knees* of the midwife.

[8] Heb., חֲרָבוֹת *(charāvōth) ruins.* There is bitter irony in the word, saying to us that while the *monuments* are stately and great, they are only mouldering away like the dead within them.

16. Oh! that I had been an untimely birth,
    Like still-born babes which never see the light.
17. For there, the wicked trouble cause no more,
    And there, the wearied ones [at last] find rest,
18. Together with them captives find repose
    And hear no more the harsh task-masters' voice.
19. The small and great alike are gathered there;
    The servant from his master is set free

H³. (page 64) chap. iii. 20-23. *Manhood lamented.*

20. Wherefore, unto the wretched, gives He light?
    Or life [prolong] to the embittered soul?
21. (To those who yearn for death that cometh not,
    And seek for it as those who treasure seek,
22. Who would rejoice with exultation—yea!
    Be glad indeed, if they could find the grave)?
23. [The grave![1]]: 'tis for the man whose way is hid,
    Whom Eloah hath hedgèd round about.

I³. (page 64) chap. iii. 24-26. *Reasons.*

24. My sighing cometh in, in place of food,
    My groanings are like water pourèd forth.
25. For, that which I so feared hath come on me,
    And what I dreaded, that hath come to me.
26. I was not careless; nor felt I secure;
    Nor rested without thought: yet, trouble came.

---

[1] That there is an *ellipsis* here is clear; the A.V. and R.V. supplying, in italics, the words: "Why is light given" from verse 20. We supply "the grave," repeating the words immediately preceding, as the thought seems to be carried over to this verse.

ELIPHAZ. FIRST ADDRESS.

k¹. (page 63) chaps. iv. and v.

k¹ | J | m | iv. 1, 2-. Apprehension.

   | n | -2. Apology.

      K | iv. 3-5. Trouble (Particular).

       L | iv. 6. Righteousness (Particular).

        M | o | iv. 7. General Proposition. ⎫

          | p | iv. 8-11. Proof. "I have ⎬ **Appeal to experience.**

          | seen." ⎭

       L | 12—v. 1.* Righteousness (General).

        M | o | v. 2. General proposition. ⎫

          | p | v. 3-5. Proof. "I have ⎬ **Appeal to experience.**

          | seen." ⎭

       K | v. 6-26.† Trouble (General).

  J | m | v. 27-. Research.

     | n | v. -27. Recommendation.

---

*L | x | iv. 12-16. Vision.

   | y | 17—v. 1. Voice. { Angelic beings 18.
Human beings 19-21.

---

†K | q | 6, 7. Trouble. Inevitable. ⎫

   | r | 8. Trust in God. ⎬ **3rd person.**

   | s | 9-16. Reason (God's greatness). ⎭

   | r | 17. Trust in God. ⎫

   | s | 18. Reason. (God's goodness). ⎬ **2nd person.**

   | q | 19-26. Trouble. Deliverance from it. ⎭

m. (page 67) chap. iv. 1, 2-.   *Apprehension.*

iv. 1. Then ELIPHAZ, the Temanite, began his reply, [1] and said :
2. If one replies to thee, [2] wouldst thou be grieved ? [3]

n. (page 67) chap. iv. -2.   *Apology.*

Yet, who from speaking can refrain himself ?

K. (page 67) chap. iv. 3-5.   *Trouble (Particular).*

3. Behold, how many others thou hast taught ;
And hast been wont to strengthen feeble hands.
4. The faltering step thy words have lifted up ;
And thou hast strengthened oft the feeble knees.
5. But now, to THEE, ⌊misfortune [4]⌋ comes, what grief ! [5]
Because it toucheth THEE, thou art dismayed !

L. (page 67) chap. iv. 6.   *Righteousness (Particular).*

6. [Ought] not thy fear [of God to be] [6] thy trust ?
And the uprightness of thy ways, thy hope ?

M. (page 67) chap. iv. 7–11.   *Appeal to experience.*

o. (p. 67) chap. iv. 7.   *General Proposition.*

7. Bethink thee ; when has the guiltless been destroyed ?
Or when were any upright ones cut off ?

p. (page 67) chap. iv. 8-11.   *Proof.*

8. I've always seen that they who evil plough [7]
And mischief sow, they ever reap the same.
9. They perish, smitten by the blast of God,
And by His angry blast [8] they are consumed.

---

[1] See note on ch. iii. 1.

[2] Heb., *try a word to thee; i,e., venture to argue or differ.*

[3] Heb., *be weary ; i.e., lose patience.*

[4] This is the noun which is to be supplied.

[5] Heb., *thou art grieved.*

[6] Thus, surely, must the *Ellipsis* be supplied.

[7] As in Prov. iii. 29.

[8] Heb., *the blast of His nostril.* Compare Psalm xviii. 15. Is. xi. 4. 2 Thes. ii. 8.

10.[1] [Hushed[2] is] the Lion's[3] roar ! [Silenced] the young
    Lion's howl !   Crushed are the strong young lion's teeth !

11. The fierce lion perisheth for lack of prey ;
    The lioness's whelps are scattered wide.

  L. (page 67) chap. iv. 12—v. 1.   *Righteousness* (*General*).

12. Now, unto me, a matter[4] was revealed ;[5]
    Mine ear did catch a whispering[6] thereof.

13. When there were thoughts, in visions of the night,
    When falls on men the vision-seeing[7] sleep.

14. Great fear did come on me, and trembling [dread]
    It made my very bones to stand in awe.

15. And then upon my face did pass a breath,[8]
    Which made my very hair to stand on end.

16. It stopped : but nothing could I then discern ;
    I looked : but no form stood before mine eyes.[9]
    But hush ! [10] For then I heard a voice[11]—[which said]—

17.   'CAN MORTAL MAN[12] BE JUST BEFORE HIS **GOD** ? [13]
    'OR BOASTFUL MAN,[14] BEFORE HIS MAKER, PURE ?

---

[1] These two verses (iv. 10, 11) are supposed by some to be spurious because the *Figure* is not seen. They are the illustration of the statement of verse 9, the wicked being compared to these animals, as in Ps. x. 9 ; xxii. 12, 13, 16, 21, &c. Verse 11 describes the effect and consequence of verse 10.

[2] By the Figure *Zeugma*, only one verb is put for three various propositions :—*broken* or *crushed.* This properly applies only to the "teeth." The other verbs must be supplied appropriate to the "roar" and "howl." We have supplied "hushed" and " silenced."

[3] No less than five words are used in this passage for lions

[4] *i.e.*, the Divine revelation concerning righteousness.

[5] Heb., disclosed *secretly* or *by steal.h*

[6] Heb. *a trifle.*

[7] Heb. תַּרְדֵּמָה (*tardeymah)* is more than any natural sleep, however deep. Compare Adam's, Gen. ii. 21 ; Abraham's, Gen. xv. 12 ; and Saul's, 1 Sam. xxvi. 12.

[8] Heb. רוּחַ (*ruach) spirit* or *breath* or *wind, i.e.,* a stirring or moving of the air caused by a being unseen.

[9] So Ginsburg's Hebrew Text ; note " So it should be," and Septuagint also.

[10] Heb. דְּמָמָה (*demamah) silence.*

[11] In Heb. the figure is *Hendiadys :* —" I heard *silence and a voice,*" *i.e.,* a whispering voice.

[12] Heb. אֱנוֹשׁ (*enōsh) man* as weak ; frail and mortal. *Not* אָדָם (*ādām) man,* as distinguished from woman ; or גֶּבֶר (*gever) man,* as mighty and strong : or, אִישׁ (*īsh) man* of high degree.

[13] Heb. *Eloah.*

[14] Heb. גֶּבֶר (*gever)*. see note above.

18. ‘ IN HIS OWN SERVANTS; LO, HE TRUSTETH NOT,
     ‘ HIS ANGELS HE DOTH CHARGE WITH IGNORANCE.[1]
19. ‘ How much more those who dwell in houses made
     ‘ Of clay; with their foundation laid in dust.[2]
     ‘ [So frail], that they are crushèd like the moth.
20. ‘ Between the morn and eve they are destroyed:
     ‘ With none to save[3]—they perish utterly.
21. ‘ Is not their life[4] within them soon removed?
     ‘ They die before to wisdom they attain.

v. 1. Call now! and is there one to answer Thee?
       To whom among the holy wilt Thou turn?

> *o.* (page 67) chap. v. 2. *General Proposition.*

2. The foolish man is killed by his own wrath;
    And indignation slays the simple ones.

> *p.* (page 67) chap. v. 3-5. *Proof.*

3. I, when I’ve seen the foolish striking root,
    Have forthwith shown [6] what would take place [and said]:
4.   ‘ His children will be far from safety set,
      ‘ And crushed to death when passing in the gate,
      ‘ With no one near at hand to rescue them.
5.   ‘ His harvest he will eat, still famishing,
      ‘ E’en though he take it from the hedge [7] of thorns.
      ‘ A snare [8] doth wait to swallow up their wealth.’

---

[1] Compare Eliphaz, chap. xv. 15.

[2] Compare chap. x. 9; xxxiii. 6; 2 Cor. v. 1.

[3] So Ginsburg’s Heb. Text and note.

[4] Heb., *tent-peg: i.e.,* their *life.* See the Oxford Gesenius, page 452, for this different reading (“ *tent-peg* ”).

[5] The question is asked in solemn irony: If none is holy and none righteous but God, Who but He can determine the standard of true righteousness.

[6] Or *pointed out,* as in Gen. xxx. 28, Isa. lxii. 2.

[7] Some MSS. read, *he takes it int the granaries.*

[8] So the R.V. The A.V. follows Kimchi.

q. (page 67) chap. v. 6, 7.   *Trouble inevitable.*

6. Be sure that evil comes not from the dust ;
   Nor trouble spring as herbage from the ground.
7. Ah no !¹   Man's trouble from his birth begins,
   Thence rises it as rise the sparks² from fire.

r. (page 67) chap. v. 8.   *Trust in GOD.*

8. But as for me I would seek unto GOD :
   Yea, before GOD would I set forth my cause ;

s. (page 67) chap. v. 9-16.   *Reason (God's greatness).*

9. Who doeth great things and unsearchable,
   And³ wondrous things till they are numberless :
10. Who giveth rain upon the thirsty⁴ earth,
    And sendeth water on the open fields.
11. Who setteth up the lowly ones on high ;
    And mourning ones He doth in safety set,
12. And doth frustrate the schemes of cunning men ;
    So that their plans they cannot bring to pass.
13. Who takes the wise in their own craftiness ;
    So that their cunning plans are all forestalled.⁵
14. [Such men] do meet with darkness in the day ;
    And at the noon-day grope, as in the night.
15. He saveth from the sword's devouring mouth,⁶
    And plucks the needy from their hand so strong.

---

¹ The ‏כִּי‎ (*kē*) is very strongly adversitive, implying the very opposite of what had just been said. It is well expressed " Ah no " by Prof. Tayler Lewis.

² Heb., *sons of the flame* (or *of the torch*).

³ So some codices with Sept., Vulg., and Syriac. See Ginsburg's Text and note.

⁴ Heb., *the face of the earth.*

⁵ Or *precipitated, i.e.,* He frustrates their plots by anticipating them, and being, as we say " beforehand with them."

⁶ Heb., *from the sword out of their mouth.* But some codices with Aramaic, Syriac, and Vulgate read *the sword of their mouth.* See note Ginsburg's Hebrew text. Thus the meaning is the same as in Ps. lvii. 4 ; lv. 21 ; lxiv. 3. Compare Isa. xlix. 2 ; Heb. iv. 12 ; Rev. i. 16 ; ii. 16 ; xix. 15. " Mouth " is put for the *edge* of the sword.

16. **Thus for the poor there comes a ground for hope ;**
    [Therefore] iniquity [1] **doth shut her mouth.** [2]

r. (page 67) chap. v. 17.   *Trust in God.*

17. **Lo ! happy is the man whom 𝔊𝔒𝔇** [3] **corrects ;** [4]
    Th' Almighty's chastening oh ! spurn thou not.

s. (page 67) **chap.** v. 18.   *Reason (God's goodness).*

18. **For He it is who wounds, yet bindeth up ;**
    He smiteth ; yet 'tis His own hands that heal.

q. (page 67) chap. v. 19-26.   *Trouble.   Deliverance from it.*

19. **In troubles six** [5] **He will deliver thee ;**
    Yea ! e'en in seven shall no misfortune harm.
20. **In famine : He will ransom thee from death ;**
    In battle, from the power [6] **of the sword,**
21. **In slander** [7] **thou shalt be in safety hid ;**
    And when destruction [8] **comes thou shalt not fear,**
22. **At devastation and at dearth thou'lt laugh ;** [9]
    And of the beasts [10] **thou shalt not be afraid.**
23. **For with the stones** [11] **thou'lt be in covenant ;**
    And e'en wild beasts shall be at peace with thee.

---

[1] *Metonymy of the Adjunct, i.e.,* "Iniquity" is put for those who work iniquity.

[2] This is the idiom for causing a thing to cease.   See Ps. cvii. 42 ; lxiii. 11.

[3] Heb., *Eloah.*

[4] Ps. xciv. 12.

[5] Heb., idiom, *six, seven,* like *once, twice,* means *ever so many.*

[6] *Metonymy* (of the Cause), "hands" being put for *power.*

[7] *Metonymy* (of *Adjunct*), *scourge of the tongue,* being put for *slander,* as in Ps. iii. 2 ; lvii. 4 ; lxiv. 3, 7, 8 ; Jer. ix. 3, 8 ; *i.e.,* when thou art slandered it shall not injure thee. So the French *coup de langue;* and German *zungendrescherei.*

[8] *Metonymy* (of *Adjunct*). *Destruction* put for the Destroyer.

[9] *Mentonymy* (of *Adjunct*), *Laugh* put for feeling *secure.*

[10] Heb., *beasts of the earth; i.e.,* wild beasts as distinct from domestic animals.

[11] *Synecdoche* (of the Species). Stones (Heb., *stones of the field*) are put for whatever makes the soil unproductive.   Verses 22, 23 are in four lines alternate, *v.* 23 explaining *v.* 22.

24. Yea, thou shalt know that peace is in thy tent;
And, looking through thy dwelling, nothing miss.

25 And thou shalt know that numerous is thy seed;
Thine offspring as the herbage of the field :[2]

26. And thou, in ripe old age unto thy grave
Shalt come; like sheaves in harvest gathered in.[3]

m. (page 67) chap. v. 27-.   *Research.*

27-. Lo! this we've pondered well; and so it is;

n. (page 67) chap. v. -27.   *Recommendation.*

-27. Hear it, and treasure it for thine own good.[4]

---

[1] Or *fold.*
[2] So the Aramaic and Septuagint. See Ginsburg's Text and note.
[3] Heb., *as stack of sheaves mounteth up in its season: i.e.,* as sheaves are piled or stacked up in the garner in harvest time.
[4] Heb., *Mark it for yourself: i.e., take it to thyself,* or, as in A.V., " for thy good."

JOB'S FIRST REPLY TO ELIPHAZ.

1'. (page 63) chap. vi. vii.

1' | N | vi. 1-7. Job's excessive grief.

O | 8-13. Death to be desired.

P | 14-21. Remonstrance. (Their feelings.)

P | 22-30. Remonstrance. (Their words.)

O | vii. 1-10. Death to be desired.

N | 11-21. Job's excessive grief.

---

vi. N. (above) chap. vi. 1-7. *Job's excessive grief.*

vi. 1. Then JOB replied, and said :—

2. Oh, that my grief could thoroughly be weighed,
And all my woe the balances uplift[1] !

3. For it would now be heavier than the sand.[2]
On this account it far outweighs my words.[3]

4. For Shaddai's arrows now [stick fast][4] in me,
The heat whereof my spirit drinketh up.
GOD'S[5] terrors now against me are arrayed.

5. Doth the wild ass bray while he is at grass ?
Or lows the ox while fodder he doth eat ?

6. Can tasteless food be eaten without salt ?
Or is there any taste in white of egg ?

---

[1] *i.e.,* If Job's woes and calamities could be put into the balances, their weight would lift up the other scale, and thus outweigh whatever might be in it.

[2] Heb., *sand of the Sea.*

[3] *i.e.,* his grief outweighs the power of language to describe it.

[4] Compare Ps. xxxviii. 2.

[5] Heb., *Eloah.*

7. [So with my grief] ; it makes my soul refuse
   All things ; as food unsavoury [1] makes one sick.

   O. (page 74) ch. vi. 8-13.   *Death to be desired.*

8. Oh, that my prayer might come [before my God] :
   That Eloah would grant my heart's desire [2]

9. That it would please Eloah me to crush ;
   That He would loose His hand and cut me off.

10. I still should comfort find ; yea, e'en in this,—
    That I could yet endure, though HE spare not—
    The Holy One,—whom [3] I have not denied.

11. But what then is my strength, that I should hope ?
    Or what mine end though I be patient [4] still ?

12. My strength ; has it become the strength of stones ?
    Or, has my flesh become like flesh of brass ?

13. [Alas !] there is not in me any help ;
    My wisdom hath been driv'n away from me.[5]

P. (page 74) chap. vi. 14-21.   *Remonstrance at his friends'* want
of sympathy.

14. E'en to the faint,[6] love still is due from friends ;
    Though he forsakes the fear of Shaddai.

15. But MY friends prove illusive, like a brook ;
    Like streams whose flowing waters disappear

16. And are not seen [7] by reason of the ice,
    [Or of the] snow, which, falling, covers them.

17. What time it waxeth warm the streams dry up ;
    When it is hot they vanish from their place.

---

[1] Heb., *sicknesses of my food.* Or, by *Hypallage, food of sickness ; i.e., food which causes sickness,* or *unsavoury food.*

[2] Heb., *my hope,* or *expectation.* Or as A.V., " the thing that *I* long for ; " *i.e., my heart's desire.*

[3] Heb., *whose words.*

[4] Heb., *prolong my soul,* or *desire.* Oxford Gesenius suggests " My patience " (661a, 6 g).   Compare R.V.

[5] *i.e.,* I am not only become helpless, but I am also become a fool, even as Eliphaz had suggested ch. v. 2.

[6] Heb., *the despairing.*

[7] Heb., *darken, i.e.,* become dark or hidden up so that they cannot be seen.

18. They turn aside from out their usual course ; [1]
    Are lost ; and gone up into empty air.[2]
19. The Caravans of Tema look about ;
    The Companies of Sheba for them long.
20. They are ashamed that they [3] had trusted them.
    They reach the spot. They stand ; and are amazed.
21. [And thus it is with you]. Ye come to me ; [4]
    Ye see a fearful sight ; and are dismayed.[5]

P. (page 74) chap. vi. 22-30. *Remonstrance at his friends' words.*

22. Came ye because I said, Give aught to me ?
    Or, Of your substance bring to me a gift ? [6]
23. Or, From the Adversary's power [7] deliver me ?
    Or, Ransom me from the oppressor's hand ?
24. Teach me, I pray ; and I will hold my peace !
    And make me understand where I have erred.
25. How forcible are words of uprightness !
    But as for YOUR words, how will THEY convince ?
26. Do YE reprove by fast'ning on MY words,
    When one who's desperate speaks [at random] like
27. The wind ? [8] Orphans ye might as well assail[9]
    And banquet on the miseries of your friend.

---

[1] Heb., *the paths of their way.*

[2] Heb., *they go up into tohu,* as in Gen. i. 2., *emptiness, i.e.,* by evaporation. This verse applies beautifully to the streams, but certainly not (as with R.V.) to Caravans ; for they can hardly be said to evaporate !

[3] So the Syriac and Aramaic. See Ginsburg's Text and note.

[4] There are various readings here. One school of Massorites has " to *him*" : *i.e.,* to your friend. Another has " to *nothing*." The Septuagint and Syriac has " to *me*." See Ginsburg's Text and note.

[5] There is a *paronamasia* here וַתִּרְאוּ ... תִּרְאוּ (*tiraū ... vattīraū*) ye see something *fearful* and *fear.* It can hardly be expressed in English.

[6] *i.e., a bribe* on my behalf.

[7] Heb., *hand* ; put by *Metonymy* for power.

[8] *i.e.,* speaks at random, as the wind seems to blow : *i.e.,* hardly knowing what he says—or whence come his words or whither they go.

[9] So Septuagint and Vulgate. See Ginsburg's text and note. Heb., *cast yourselves upon* as in Gen. xliii. 18. There is no occasion to supply " *lots* " as in the R.V.

28. Now, therefore, be content, and look on me.
'Twill be before your face[3] if I should lie,

29. Return, I pray you; let not wrong prevail ;
Yea, turn again; my cause is truly just.

30. Is there, I ask, perverseness in my tongue ?
And can I not discern[4] iniquity ?

O. (page 74) ch. vii. 1-10.　*Death to be desired.*

vii. 1. Is not a mortal's life a warfare on the earth ?
And as a hireling's day, his days?

2. As [weary] labourer panteth for the shade,
And as the hireling longeth for his wage,

3. So I inherit months of vanity ;
And nights of weariness have been my lot.[5]

4. As soon as I lie down to sleep, I say :
'How long till I arise, and night be gone ? '
And I am full of tossings till the dawn.

5. My flesh is clothed with worms and clods of earth,
My broken skin heals up ; then runs afresh.

6. Swifter than weaver's shuttle are my days,
And they are spent without a gleam of hope.

7. Remember Thou,[6] that life is but a breath,
Mine eye shall not again behold[7] the good.

---

[1] *i.e.,* evident to you. The line might run : " Surely I'll not deceive you to your face."

[2] Heb., חך *(chaik) the palate : i.e.,* as the palate discerns the different tastes of food, so, Cannot I discern what is wrong and what is right.

[3] Heb., *they have prepared.* This idiom is frequently found, referring to some unknown and invisible agencies which carry out God's judgments. Compare Ps. xlix. 15, " like sheep *they* thrust them (the wicked) into Sheol." So Job iv. 19; xviii 18; xix. 26; xxxiv. 20. The idiom passes into the New Testament, Luke xii. 20, " *they* demand thy soul of thee." In an opposite sense we have Isa. lx. 11, " *they* shall keep thy gates open." It may therefore be well rendered as *impersonal.*

[4] Job turns now to God, and addresses Him. Compare ch. xiii. 20.

[5] *i.e., enjoy.* I shall no more enjoy good things.

8. The eyes that see me now, will see no more,
   But Thine shall see me, though I shall not be.
9. As wasted cloud that vanishes away,
   So he that goeth to Sheōl comes not up.
10. No more doth he return unto his house.
   The place that knew him, knoweth him no more.

N. (page 74) chap. vii. 11-21. *Job's excessive grief.*

11. [And hence my grief]. I can't restrain my words ;
   In anguish of my spirit I must speak,
   And utt'rance find for bitterness of soul.
12. Am I a [restless] sea ? or, of the deep,
   A monster, that o'er me Thou sett'st a watch ?
13. I said, ' My bed to me shall comfort bring ;
   ' My couch may help to take away my grief.'
14. Then Thou dost terrify my sleep with dreams,
   And with dread visions fill me with alarm,
15. So that my soul e'en strangling would prefer—
   Death [self-inflicted, wrought]—by mine own hands. [1]
16. I loathe myself : I would not thus live on.
   Oh ! let me, then, alone ; my days are vanity.
17. What is frail man[2] that Thou shouldst nurture him ? [3]
   Or that Thou shouldest set Thy heart on him.
18. That every morning[4] Thou should'st visit him,
   [And then] at other times [5] should'st try him sore?
19. How long ! Wilt Thou not turn[6] away from me ?
   Wilt Thou not for one instant[7] let me be ?

---

[1] Heb., *from my own bones,* "bones" being put by *Metonymy* for *limbs.* Death by self-strangulation is the thought.

[2] Heb., *Enosh.* See note, chap. iv. 17.

[3] Or *bring him up.* Is. i. 2.

[4] Heb., *at mornings.* Psalm lxxiii. 14.

[5] Heb., *at moments.* See Ps. xi. 4, 5.

[6] Compare ch. xiv. 6.

[7] Heb. *till I swallow my spittle.* An Arabic idiom, *for one instant ;* Just as we say "The twinkling of an eye " to express the same idea.

20. Watcher of men, what do I unto Thee,
    If I have sinned, why set me as Thy butt?
    As if I were a burden unto Thee.[1]
21. Why, rather, dost Thou not forgive my sin,
    And take away all mine iniquity?
    For, in the dust, I soon shall lay me down;
    And thou shalt seek me, but I shall not be.

---

[1] The current printed Heb. Text reads *unto myself*. But this is one of the emendations of the *Sopherim*; who, by dropping the letter (*caph*), changed the primitive reading "Thee" to "me." See note on chap. i. 5.

BILDAD'S FIRST ADDRESS.

k² (page 63) chap. viii.

k² | Q | viii. 1, 2.   Reproof of Job.
    | R | 3.   Appeal to Reason.
        | S | 4-7.   Application to Job.
     | R | 8-19.   Appeal to Tradition.
        | S | 20.   Application to Job.
    | Q | 21, 22.   Comfort for Job.

Q. (above) chap. viii. 1, 2.   *Reproof of Job.*

viii. 1. Then answered BILDAD the Shuite said :—
   2. How long wilt thou pour forth¹ such² words as these ?
     [How long] shall they be like the blustering wind ?

R. (above) chap. viii. 3.   *Appeal to reason.*

   3. The [righteous]³ GOD : Doth He in judgment err ?
     Or, Shaddai : Doth He pervert the right ?

S. (above) chap. viii. 4-7.   *Application to Job.*

   4. It may be that thy SONS⁴ 'gainst Him have sinned ;
     And He, for THEIR transgression, cut them off.⁵
   5. If thou thyself would'st now seek unto GOD⁶
     And supplication make⁷ to Shaddai ;
   6. If thou thyself wert only right and pure,
     Then surely He would hear thine earnest prayer⁸
     And prosperous make thy righteous dwelling place.⁹

---

¹ Heb., *speak*, or *babble*.

² Heb., *these* [things].

³ Heb., *El.*   The word *righteous* may be well supplied from the next line.

⁴ Or, *It may be that thy sons have sinned ; i.e.,* if not thyself it may be they.

⁵ Heb., *by the hand of their transgression.* See R.V., and A.V. margin.

⁶ Heb., *El.*

⁷ We might say *earnest prayer*, because the Heb., תִּתְחַנָּן (*tith-channan*), being in the Hithpael is intensive and reflexive, and means *to seek to make God gracious to one's self.*

⁸ So it should be with Septuagint. See Ginsburg's Heb. text and note.

⁹ Heb., *thy habitation of righteousness.* This, by the figure *Enallage*, means *thy righteous habitation.*

7. However small might seem thy first estate,
   Thy latter end should be exceeding great.

R. (page 80) chap. viii. 8-19. *Appeal to Tradition.*

8. Enquire, I pray thee, of the former age ;
   And of their fathers, set thyself to learn,
9. (For we're of yesterday, and nothing know ;
   Yea, as a shadow are our days on earth).
10. Shall THEY not [1] speak to thee, and to thee tell [2]
    Wise things [3] from their experience [4] [such as these]?
11.   ' The reed : can it grow high without the mire ?
       ' The flag : can it thrive where no water is ?
12.   ' While yet 'tis green, and while it stands uncut,
       ' Sooner than any grass 'tis withered up.
13.   ' So is the end [5] of all who GOD [6] forget ;
       ' So perisheth the hope of godless men.
14.   ' His confidence shall worthless prove [7] to him ;
       ' And that on which he trusts,[8] a spider's web.
15.   ' He leans upon his tent—it giveth way,[9]
       ' He clings to it ; but it will not endure.
16.   ' [Or like the Tree] [10] so green before the sun,
       ' Whose boughs spread forth o'er all his garden-bed ;

---

[1] The Figure of *Erotesis* putting an emphatic assertion by way of question ; meaning *they shall* INDEED. Compare Ruth ii. 9.

[2] See note Ginsburg's Hebrew Text.

[3] Heb. מִלִּים (*millīm*) not merely *words* but *sententious words, sayings, parables, adages,* such as those that follow :—*e.g.,* the *reed,* the *flag,* the *spider,* the *tree,* and the application of them by the men of the former generation themselves.

[4] Heb. *from their heart.* But it does not here refer merely to *feeling.*

Not *heart-felt,* but rather *heart-known* : *i.e.,* understanding and experience.

[5] So the Septuagint. See Ginsburg's Heb. Text and note.

[6] Heb., *El.*

[7] Heb. יָקוֹט (*yakot*), *shall disgust him ;* or *shall become or show itself worthless to him.*

[8] Heb., his *trust,* put by *Metonymy,* for *that on which he trusts.*

[9] Heb., *it standeth not.*

[10] It is clear that the *Ellipsis* must be thus supplied.

17.   'Beside the fountain[1] are its roots entwined ;
    'It overtops[2] the [lofty] house of stone,[3]
18.   'If one uproot it from its place, it[4] doth
    'At once disown him, with " I know thee not."
19.   'Behold [thus ends] the joy of its brief life[5]
    'While, where it grew[6] shall other trees spring up.'

    S. (page 80) chap. viii. 20.   *Application to Job.*

20.   But upright men GOD[7] never casts away ;
      Nor takes He by the hand the evil doers.

    Q. (page 80) chap. viii. 21, 22.   *Comfort for Job.*

21. [Then wait] ; and[8] He'll thy mouth with laughter fill,
    And also fill thy lips with shouts of joy.
22. [While] they who hate thee shall be clothed with shame,
    And tents of wicked men be seen no more.

---

[1] So לַג is rendered "fountain" in Song iv. 12, where it associated with garden.

[2] Heb., *overlooks : i.e., overtops.*

[3] Heb., אֶבֶן *stones (ĕvĕn) a stone* is used by *Metonymy* for anything made of stone ; *e.g.,* a *statue, vessels* (Ex. vii. 19), *stone-troughs, weights* (De. xxv. 13): and compare the Eng. weight of 14lbs. called a *stone.* It is from the root בָּנָה *(banah),*

to *build ;* hence, *stones used for building* (1 Kings x. 2, 11).

[4] *i.e.,* the place saith to the Tree.

[5] Heb., *the joy of his way,* as A.V. and R.V.

[6] Heb., *from the dust, earth ; i.e.,* the soil where the uprooted tree had grown.

[7] Heb., *El.*

[8] Or, *until.*

JOB'S FIRST REPLY TO BILDAD.

1². (page 63) chap. ix., x.

1² | T | ix.   Answer to Bildad.
    | U | x.   Expostulation with God.

———

T. (page 83) chap. ix.   *Answer to Bildad.*

T | V¹ | ix. 1-4.   Job unable to answer.

W | t | 5-10.   God's power.   Works un-⎫
    | | searchable.   ⎪
    | | ⎬ General.
    | u | 11, 12.   God's dealings.   Ways ⎪
    | | inscrutable.   ⎭

V² | 13-18.   Job unable to answer.

W | t | 19-24.   God's exercise of power⎫
    | | Unequal.   ⎬ Personal.
    | u | 25-31.   God's dealings.   Unequal.⎭

V³ | 32-35.   Job unable to answer.

V¹. (page 83) chap. ix. 1-4.   *Job unable to answer Bildad.*

ix. 1. Then answered JOB, and said :
    2. Most surely do I know that this is so ;
        But, how can mortal man¹ be just with GOD ?

    3. If man contend in argument with HIM,
        Of thousand things he could not answer one.
    4. However wise of heart, and stout of limb,
        Who ever bravèd HIM, and prosperèd.

    t. (page 83) chap ix. 5-10.   *God s power.   His works
        unsearchable.   (General.)*

    5. Who moves the mountains, and they know it not ;
        Who overturneth them in His fierce wrath ;
    6. Who makes the Earth to tremble from her place,
        So that the pillars thereof rock themselves.
    7. Who bids the sun, and it withholds its light,²
        And round about the stars he sets a seal.
    8. Who arch'd the heavens³ by Himself⁴ alone,
        And marcheth on upon the cloudy⁵ heights.
    9. Who made the Fold,⁶ Orion⁷, and Pleiades,⁸
        The hidden [stars in] spaces⁹ of the South.
    10. Who doeth mighty works, past finding out,
        And wondrous things, in number infinite.

---

¹ Heb.,   *Enosh.*   See note on ch. iv. 17.

² Josh. x. 12.

³ Heb. *He bent the heavens ; i.e.,* the *arch* of heaven over head.

⁴ So Isa. xlix. 24.

⁵ The celebrated " Mugah " Codex reads *the clouds.* (See note, Ginsburg's Heb. Text.) *The heights of the clouds,* would mean, therefore, *cloudy heights.* This keeps the harmony of the context. In *vv.* 5 and 6 we have the earth ; and in *vv.* 7-9 we have the heavens. " The sea " here breaks up the sequence of thought. Compare Isa. xiv. 14.

⁶ Heb., עָשׁ *(ash).* The A.V. renders it " Arcturus." The R.V. " the Bear." The Stars and Constellations and Signs, were *named* and *numbered* by God, their Creator. See Isa. xl. 26, and Ps. cxlvii. 4. In ch. xxxviii. 31, 32 (עַשׁ *aish*), and Amos v. 8 we have two of these again. This name of the Constellation has suffered in its transmission through the ages. The Hebrew *Ash* is preserved in the Arabic

u. (page 83) chap. ix. 11, 12.   *God's dealings.   His ways inscrutable (General.)*

11. Behold ! He passeth, but I see Him not ;
    He sweepeth by, but is invisible.

12. Lo, He doth seize ; who then can hold Him back ? [1]
    Or, who shall say to Him ' What doest Thou ? '

V². (page 83) chap. ix. 13-18.   *Job unable to answer.*

13. Eloah will not turn back from His wrath
    Till proud confederates [2] stoop beneath His hand.

14. How then can I [address or] answer [3] Him ?
    Or choose my words [for argument] with Him ?

15. I could not be induced [4] to make reply,
    Though just : But I would supplicate my Judge.

16. If I had called, and He had answered me,
    I could not then feel sure that He had heard— [5]

17. He who o'erwhelms me with [destructive] storm,
    And multiplies my wounds without a cause :

18. Who hardly suffers me to take my breath,
    But fills me with exceeding bitterness. [6]

---

name *Al Naish* or *Annaish* (the Assembled). The brightest star in it has come down to us with the name *Dubhe*, which means *a flock.* The change, doubtless, arose from the confusion between the Hebrew *Dohver, a fold ;* and *Dohv, a bear.* No Bear is found pictured in any of the Ancient Zodiacs ; and no Bear was ever seen with a long tail ! The names of the other stars in this Constellation are all cognate, and in harmony with the central truth conveyed ; *e.g.*, " Merach " (Heb., *the flock ;* Arabic, *purchased*). "Phaeda" *guarded* or *numbered.* "Alioth," *a she goat ;* "Al Kaid," *the assembled ;* " El Alcola," *the sheepfold.* Not one has a name that does not agree with the others. (See *The Witness of the Stars,* pp. 152-157, by the same author and publisher.)

[7] Heb., כְּסִיל (*Cesîl*) *a strong one.* The constellation now known as Orion. In the Denderah Zodiac his name is *Ha-ga-t : i.e., he who triumphs.* And the hieroglyphic characters read *Oar.* Orion was anciently spelt *Oarion*, probably from the Hebrew root *Or*, which means *light.* The ancient Akkadian name was *Ur-and, the light of heaven.*

[8] Heb., כִּימָה (*Cimah*) *the cluster* of stars in the Sign *Taurus.* It means *the congregated* or *assembled.* The Syriac name is *Succoth*, which means *booths.* (See *The Witness of the Stars,* p. 124, by the same author and publisher.)

[9] Heb., *chambers.*

[1] Heb., *cause Him to turn back.*

[2] Heb., *helpers of pride, i.e.,* by *Enallage, proud helpers,* those who

t. (page 83) chap. ix. 19-24.   *God's exercise of power unequal.*
(*Personal.*)

19. If I appeal to strength ; Lo ! He is strong.
    And if to justice ; Who could summon Him ? ₁

20. Should I attempt to justify myself,
    My mouth would instantly the act condemn.²

21. If I should say, ' My heart and life are pure,'
    My self conceit would prove me the reverse.
    I do [indeed] despise [and loathe] myself.³

22. 'Tis all the same : therefore I say it out :
    The good and wicked he [alike] destroys.

23. If pestilential scourge slays suddenly,
    He mocketh at the trouble of the good !

24. The Earth is ruled o'er by a lawless one ;
    The faces of its judges He doth veil ;
    If not ; then, Who is it [that doth all this] ?

u. (page 83) chap. ix. 25-31. *God's dealings unequal. (Personal.)*

25. My [happy] days ⁴ [ran] swifter than a post,⁵
    They fled apace ; as if no good they saw.

26. They passèd by like swift papyrus boat,⁶
    Or as the vulture pounceth on its food.

---

help each other, confederate against God.

³ The verb means *to address* as well as *to answer.* So we have introduced both words.

⁴ See note, Ginsburg's Heb. text.

⁵ *i.e.,* as my troubles had come without a cause, I should have considered their removal to be causeless also.

⁶ Heb., *bitternesses*: The *plural* being put by *Hiberosis* for the singular denoting the superlative of kind and degree.

¹ See note, Ginsburg's Heb. Text. The R.V. has the same sense by supplying "who [saith He] will summon me ? "

² Heb., It or He would prove me perverse.

³ Heb., *my soul.*

⁴ *i.e.,* my former happy days. Some Codices, with Septuagint, omit " therefore." See note Ginsburg's Heb. Text.

⁵ Heb., *a runner.* Hence we may supply the verb *ran.*

⁶ Translators give various renderings according to the root from which they derive אֵבָה (*evah*). Some "vessels of bulrush " from אֵב, (*ev*) : others "vessels of desire," from אָבָה, *ahvah, i.e.,* desiring to reach their haven : others "vessels of hostility " (from אֵיבָה, *eyvah, enmity*) : *i.e.,* pirate vessels. Others identify it with *Abai,* an Abyssinian name for the Nile ; others with *Joppa.*

27. If I should say
> 'I will forget my grief,
> 'Cast off my heaviness and brighten up,'
28. Then, with a shudder, I recall my woe.
I know Thou wilt not hold me innocent;
29. [Thou wilt] account me guilty.[1] [Be it so];
Then wherefore should I labour thus in vain?
30. E'en though I bathe in water pure as snow,
And wash my hands [and make them] clean with soap;[2]
31. E'en then thou wouldest plunge me in the ditch;
And make me an abhorrence to my clothes.[3]

V[3]. (page 83) chap. ix. 32-35.   *Job unable to answer.*

32. For He is not a man like me, that I
Should say, 'Let us together, come, and plead!'
33. Oh! that there were[4] an Arbiter[5] with us,
One who could put His hand upon us both!
34. Oh! that He would remove, from me, His rod,
So that His terror might not make me fear:
35. Then could I speak, and boldly plead my cause:
But now, [alas], it is not so with me.

---

[1] Heb., *I shall be accounted guilty.* Our rendering though in the second person expresses exactly the same thought.

[2] The Heb. denotes *soap* as well as *lye.*

[3] *i.e.*, regarding himself as still naked, his clothes are personified as abhorring him.

[4] So some Codices and Septuagint. See note Ginsburg's Heb. Text.

[5] See Tregelles's Gesenius.

U. (page 83) chap. x.   *Job's expostulation with God.*

U | Y | x. 1, 2.   Petition.

Z | v | 3-7.   Expostulation.   God's power.
    | w | 8-13.   His creature.

Z | v | 14-17.   Expostulation.   God's ways.
    | w | 18, 19.   His creature.

Y | 20-22.   Petition.

––––––––––

Y. (above) chap. x. 1, 2.   *Petition.*

x. 1. My soul is weary of my [wretched] life ;
    I yield myself unto my inward grief ;
    I must tell out my bitterness of soul :

2. And to Eloah say, Condemn me not ;
    But make it known why Thou dost strive with me.

v. (above) chap. x. 3-7.   *Expostulation.   God's power.*

3. Is it a pleasure[1] that Thou should'st oppress ?
    And thus despise the labour of Thy hands,
    And prosper [all] the schemes of wicked men ?

4. Hast Thou then eyes of flesh [like mortal man] ?[2]
    Dost Thou behold indeed as he[3] beholds ?

5. Are Thy days like the days of mortal man ?[3]
    Or like the days of mighty man,[4] Thy years ?

6. That Thou shouldst seek for mine iniquity,
    And for my sin shouldst [diligently] search ?

––––––––––

[1] Heb., *good.*
[2] Supplying the *Ellipsis* from the next line.

[3] Heb., *Enōsh.*   See note on ch. iv. 17.
[4] Heb., *Gibbōr.*   See note on ch. iv. 17.

7. For Thou must know I'm not [this] guilty man.
But from Thy hand none can deliver me.

w. (page 88) chap. x. 8-13. *His creature.*

8. Still Thine own hands have framed and fashioned me,
Behind, before ¹ : Yet me Thou hast destroyed !

9. Remember, that as clay Thou didst me mould ;
And wilt Thou turn me back again to dust ?

10. Didst Thou not pour me forth like milk ?
And make me to coagulate like cheese ? ²

11. With skin and flesh hast Thou not clothèd me ? ³
With bones and sinews strengthenèd my frame ?

12. Both life and favour ⁴ Thou hast given to me ; ⁵
Thy watchful providence preserved my breath.

13. Yet these things ⁶ Thou wast planning in Thy heart.
For, long ago the thought had dwelt with Thee.⁷

v. (page 88) chap. x. 14-17. *Expostulation. God's Ways.*

14. If I had sinned, Thou wouldst have marked it,
And not acquitted me from conscious guilt.

15. Had I been wicked, woe is unto me !
Yet, though I'm just, I may not lift my head ;
So full of shame am I. Look on my misery.

16. And should I [dare to] lift it,⁸ then wouldst Thou,
Like howling lion still pursue my soul,⁹
And still against me show Thy wondrous power.

17. Against me Thou wouldst bring new witnesses,
Thine indignation towards me would increase,
Troop after troop¹⁰ against me they¹¹ would come.

---

¹ Heb. *round about.*
² Referring to the development of the embryo.
³ Compare Ps. cxxxix. 14-16.
⁴ " Life and favour." This expression occurs only here.
⁵ Heb., *done to me.*

⁶ *i.e.*, these punishments.
⁷ Heb., *with thee.* Compare 1 Kings xi. 11.
⁸ Heb., *lift itself up.*
⁹ *i.e.*, *me.*
¹⁰ Heb., *relays, reinforcement* . .
¹¹ *i.e.*, these witnesses.

w. (page 88), chap. x. 18, 19. *His creature.*

18. Then wherefore didst Thou bring me from the womb ?
I might have died, and no eye looked on me.
19. I should have been as if I had not been ;
And from the womb been carried to the grave. [1]

Y. (page 88), chap. x. 20-22. *Petition.*

20. How few my days ! Oh ! let Him[2] then desist,
And leave me, that I may some comfort take,
21. Before I go whence I shall not return,
Into the darkness[3] and the shades of death,
22. A land of darkness, dark as darkest night.
The land of death-shade, where no order reigns,
And where the day is like the midnight—dark.

---

[1] Compare ch. iii. 11-13.
[2] So the Heb. marginal reading called *K'thiv.*

[3] Heb., *a land of darkness,* **as in** the next line.

ZOPHAR'S FIRST ADDRESS.

k³. (page 63) chap. xi.

k³ | A | xi. 1-6. Rebuke. God's judgments (particular) on Job.

    B | a | 7, 8. Human ignorance.
       | b | 9-12. Divine knowledge.

    B | a | 13. Human merit.
       | b | 14-19. Divine reward.

  A | 20. Rebuke. God's judgments (general) on the wicked.

A. (above), chap. xi. 1-6. *Rebuke. God's judgments. (Particular) on Job.*

xi. 1. Then answered ZOPHAR, the Naamathite, and said:
2. Will not a mass of words[1] admit reply?
And must a man of lips![2] perforce be right?
3. Thy talk may put to silence mortal MEN;
THEM thou may'st mock, none putting thee to shame.
4. Thou maỳest say indeed to one of THEM,
' Pure is my doctrine: In His [3] eyes I'm clean.'
5. But, oh! that Eloah would speak to thee;
HIS lips unclose; and speaking, stop thy mouth,
6. And show thee some of wisdom's secret depths,
That they are far beyond [4] all that is seen.

---

[1] Heb., *a multitude of words.* Alluding to the length of Job's reply.
[2] Heb., *a man of lips*: *i.e.*, a man of many words. In contradistinction to Ex. iv. 10.
[3] So it should be according to Ginsburg's Heb. text and Septuagint.

[4] Heb., *double*: perhaps meaning *manifold* as in R.V. Or, that beyond what is actually "seen" there is also much to be learned which is not seen: *i.e.*, a Divine meaning beyond the outward appearance. See the Oxford Gesenius p. 695 b.

> Then wouldst thou know that ☉☉☉ [1] exacteth [2] less
> Than all that thine iniquity deserves.

a. (page 91) chap. xi. 7, 8. *Human Ignorance.*

7. Eloah's wisdom deep ; canst thou search out ? [3]
   Lo, Shaddai's [4] perfect way canst thou attain ?
8. 'Tis high as heaven's heights : What can'st thou do ?
   Deeper than Sheol's depths : What can'st thou know ?

b. (page 91) chap. xi. 9-12. *Divine Knowledge.*

9. Its measurement is longer than the Earth ;
   [Its breadth is] broader than the sea.
10. If He pass by, and makes arrest,[5] or should
    To judgment call ; [6] Who then shall Him resist ?
11. For well He knows the vanity of men : [7]
    And marks their sin, though seeming not to heed.
12. But vain man is of understanding [8] void,
    Yea, man is born like a wild ass's colt.

a. (page 91) chap. xi. 13. *Human Merit.*

13. [But as for thee] : Hadst thou prepared thy heart,
    And stretchèd forth thy hands to him in prayer :

b. (page 91) chap. xi. 14-19. *Divine Reward.*

14. If sin were in thy hand, 'twould be forgiv'n [9] ;
    Evil had been removèd from thy tent,[10]

---

[1] Heb., *Eloah.*

[2] Heb., נָשָׁה (*nāshāh*) *to sink.* Hence, to forget (Gen. xli. 51) ; and, where sin is forgotten, it is forgiven (Ps. xxxii. 1). But money is *sunk* as well as memory of past events. Money *lent* is often *forgotten* by the debtors. Hence it means also *to lend* and is thus associated with *usury* and of *exacting* payment. The A.V. is therefore correct here. See R.V. marg.

[3] 1 Cor. ii. 10.

[4] The emphasis is on these **Divine** titles.

[5] Heb., *deliver over : i.e.,* arrest.

[6] Heb., *cause to assemble: i.e.,* call the assembly for judgment.

[7] Heb., *mortals of vanity.*

[8] Heb., *a heart.* Compare Prov. vi. 33. Hos. iv. 11.

[9] Heb. *put away.*

[10] According to some Codices with Aramaic, Sept., Syr., and Vulg, read *tent.* See Ginsburg's Heb. Text and note.

15. Thou wouldst thy face uplift without a stain ;
    Yea, firm, thou wouldèst stand, and need not fear :
16. For all thy misery thou wouldst then[1] forget ;
    Or think of it as waters passed away.[2]
17. Brighter than noon-day would thy future[3] be ;
    And what is darkness now would be like morn.
18. Thou wouldst have confidence ; for there is hope ;
    And having looked around, might rest secure ;
19. And lay thee down, with none to make afraid,
    [But rather fear thee], and thy favour seek.

A. (page 91) chap. xi. 20. *Rebuke.   God's judgments (general)
on the wicked.*

20. But as for wicked men, their eyes will fail,[4]
    And every refuge to them useless prove,
    Their hope will vanish [5] like a puff of breath. [6]

---

[1] Or "now," according to note in Ginsburg's Heb. Text, and Syriac version.

[2] Or, Like waters passed away, thou'lt think of it no more.

[3] Heb. חֶלֶד (*cheled*) like the Greek αἰών (*aiōn*) age, or time in passing ; well represented here by *future*, referring to *time*, rather than to life.

[4] Heb., *consume* : *i.e.*, with longing.

[5] Heb., *hath perished.*

[6] So A.V. margin.

JOB'S FIRST REPLY TO ZOPHAR.

1³. (page 63) chaps. xii.—xiv.

1³ | C | xii. 1-4. Non-inferiority of Job to his friends.
    | D | 5-12. Job's appeal to his friends.
    | E | 13-25. God. Job declares Him.
    | C | xiii. 1-5. Non-inferiority of Job to his friends.
    | D | 6-18. Job's appeal to his friends.
    | E | xiii. 19—xiv. 22. God. Job appeals to Him.

C. (above) chap. xii. 1-4. *Non-inferiority of Job to his friends.*

xii. 1. Then answered JOB, and said :
    2. Ye are the people : not a doubt of that :
       And, as for wisdom, it will die with you :
    3. But I have intellect as well as you ;
       And I am not inferior to you :
       Who hath not knowledge of such things as these ?
    4. Sport to his friends ! And have I come to this !
       Ev'n I, who call on **GOD**,[1] and whom He hears,
       A just, a perfect man to be your sport.[2]

D. (above) chap. xii. 5-12. *Job's appeal to his friends.*

    5. A lamp's [3] despised by one who feels he's safe ; [4]
       But 'tis prepared [5] for them of tottering feet.

---

[1] Heb., *Eloah.*

[2] Perhaps in allusion to Zophar's comparison in ch. xi. 12.

[3] Heb., לַפִּיד (*lappīd*) *a lamp.* Modern commentators, making no sense of this, take the liberty of dividing the word, לְ *for*, and פִּיד (*pīd*) *misfortune* or *calamity.* But there is no occasion thus to treat the word.

[4] Heb., שַׁאֲנָן (*shāhan*) *to rest, without care.* Comp. Is. xxxiii. 20, *quiet.*

[5] Heb., Niphal participle, as in Gen. xli. 32 (marg.), Neh. viii. 10. Ps. lvii. 7 (marg).

6. Prosp'rous and peaceful are the spoilers' tents;
    Security is theirs who GOD [1] provoke:
    Abundance doth Eloah [2] give to them.

7. Indeed, ask now the beasts: they [3] thee shall teach;
    The birds of heav'n shall thee instruction give.

8. Hold converse with the Earth, and it will speak;
    Yea, fishes of the sea will tell the same.[4]

9. Who knoweth not by every one of these,
    That 'tis Jehovah's [5] hand that doeth this?

10. In whose hand lieth every living soul,
    The spirit of all flesh,—of every man.

11. Doth not the ear discern the sense of words,
    Just as the palate doth distinguish food?

12. So with the aged there is wisdom found,
    And length of days doth understanding give.

E. (page 94) chap. xii. 13-25.   *God. Job declares Him.*

13. With HIM,[6] then, there must wisdom be, and might;
    Counsel [to plan] and wisdom [to adapt].

14. Lo! He casts down, and it cannot be raised;
    He shutteth up and no man openeth.

15. The waters He withholds; the streams run dry;
    He sends them forth, they devastate the earth.

16. To Him [belong] both strength and wisdom's might,
    To Him [are known] deceivers [7] and deceived;

17. 'Tis He who leadeth counsellors, from whom
    He wisdom strips; and maketh judges fools.

---

[1] Heb., *El.*

[2] The use of *Eloah* here seems to forbid the rendering of some who translate, "who bringeth a God in his hand."

[3] Heb., *it, i.e.,* every one of them.

[4] Heb., *to thee.*

[5] Some codices read *Eloah.* See Ginsburg's Heb. Text and note.

[6] *i.e., God.* The omission of the name increases the emphasis here; while the pronoun עִמּוֹ *(immō), with Him,* is very emphatic and solemn.

[7] Heb., *deceiver.*

18. 'Tis He who breaks [confed'rate] bonds [1] of kings,
    And girds their loins with cords [as captives led];

19. He leadeth priests [2] [of their pretentions] stripped,
    And overthrows the long-established [3] [thrones].

20. The trusted [speaker] He deprives of speech;
    And takes away discernment from the old.

21. 'Tis He who doth on princes pour contempt;
    And strippeth of their strength[4] [the stout] and strong.

22. Deep things from out of darkness He reveals;
    Yea, bringeth things to light from out death's shade.[5]

23. He maketh nations great; and then destroys;
    Increaseth them;[6] and then, doth captive lead.

24. Of reason He deprives the princes of the Earth,
    And makes them wander in a pathless waste.[7]

25. They grope in darkness, as in densest night,[8]
    Therefore, they stagger like a drunken man.

C. (page 94) ch. xiii. 1-5.   *Non-inferiority of Job to his Friends.*

xiii. 1. Behold, all these things [9] mine own eye hath seen,
    Mine ear hath heard; and understood them all.

2. What ye know, I know also, even I :
    In no one thing do I fall short of you.

---

[1] Not necessarily literal *bonds* of iron, but bonds of alliance ; *i.e.,* confederacies of kings.

[2] Heb., כֹּהֲנִים *(cohanim) priests*, as R.V. Not " princes " as A.V.

[3] The word means *firmly enduring ; i.e., perpetual,* surviving the changes of time. Hence it is applied to perennial water ; or to rocks (Jer. xlix. 19 ; l. 44 ; or to nations (Jer. v. 15). So here we may apply it to thrones.

[4] Heb., *looseneth the girdle of the strong,* which is the idiom for depriving of strength, because it disables the wearer for the contest by letting the garments fly loose, and thus hindering the necessary movement for the putting forth of strength.

[5] Heb., צַלְמָוֶת *(tzalmáveth), the shadow of death.* A word which, with *Sheol* and *Hades,* should be Anglicised.

[6] Heb., *spreadeth out.*

[7] Heb., תֹהוּ *(tohu)* Gen. i. 2.

[8] Heb., *and no light, i.e., without light.*

[9] So some codices with Syriac and Vulgate. See Ginsburg's Heb. text and note. Compare xxxiii. 29.

3. It is to Shaddai that I would speak ;
   With GOD [1] to reason, that is my desire.
4. But as for YOU, framers of lies [2] are YE ;
   Physicians of no value [3] are ye all.
5. Would that ye altogether held your peace ;
   That, of itself, would show that ye are wise.

D. (page 94) ch. xiii. 6-18. *Job's appeal to his Friends.*

6. But hear, I pray, the reasoning of my mouth, [4]
   And to the pleadings of my lips attend.
7. Is it for GOD [1] ye utter what is wrong ?
   Is it on His behalf ye speak deceit ?
8. Dare ye show partiality to Him ? [5]
   Is it, indeed, for GOD [1] that ye contend ?
9. Would it be well that He should search you out ?
   Or can ye mock at Him, as at frail man ?
10. Be sure, that you, He'll openly convict [6]
    If you in partiality acquit.
11. Should not His majesty make you afraid ?
    And should not dread of Him upon you fall ?
12. Your weightiest words [7] are as the ashes [8] —light ;
    Your arguments, like clay defences—weak.
13. Hold ye your peace ; let me alone, that I
    May speak,—and then let come on me what will.

---

[1] Heb., *El.*

[2] Oxford Gesenius : " Ye are falsehood-plasterers."

[3] Heb., *Physicians of vanity.*

[4] So the Septuagint. See Ginsburg's Text and note.

[5] Heb., *lift up His countenance ; i.e.,* accept His person by showing Him favour and patronising Him.

[6] The *Polyptoton* is emphatic, *convicting he will convict.* The emphasis

implies not merely certainty but **sets** it in contrast with the secrecy of **the** next line.

[7] Heb., זִכְרֹנֵיכֶם (*zikronieykem*) *memorable sayings, wise saws, apophegms, grave maxims.* We have rendered it weighty because the contrast is with the lightness of *dust.*

[8] Heb., *parables of ashes,* so called because of their lightness and incoherency.

14. Aye, come what may, the risk I willingly
    Will take;[1] and put my life into my hand.[2]

15. Though He may slay me, [yet] for Him[3] I'll wait;
    And before Him my doings would defend.

16. Yes, even He shall my salvation be,
    For none impure shall stand before His face.

17. Hear now [my friends] give heed[4] unto my word,
    And keep my declaration in your ears.

18. Behold now, I have orderèd my cause ;
    I know that I shall be declarèd just.

E. (page 94) ch. xiii. 19—xiv. 22. *God.*[5] *Job's Appeal to Him.*

19. Who then is he[6] that will contend with me ?
    For now, if I keep silence, I should die.

20. Only [O God] two things do not to me ;
    And then I will not hide me from Thy face:

21. Thy hand—from off me—take Thou far away,
    Nor let Thy terror fill me with alarm.

22. Then call Thou [me, and] I will answer [Thee] ;
    Or, I will speak, and do Thou answer ME.[7]

23. How many are my sins,—iniquities—
    Transgressions ?—These, oh ! make Thou me to know.

24. Why hidest Thou from me Thy countenance ?
    Why shouldst Thou count me as Thine enemy ?

---

[1] Two Hebrew idioms expressing great risk. The former is difficult to explain ; the latter being an English idiom also, we have retained.

[2] Some codices with Sept., Syr. and Vulg. read *hands* (pl.). See Ginsburg's Text and note.

[3] Text *written* " not" (which R.V. follows), but in margin to be *read* "for Him" (which A.V. follows). Some codices, with Aramaic, Syr. and Vulg. with one early printed edition both *write* and *read* "*for Him.*" See Ginsburg's Heb. Text and note.

[4] The Figure *Polyptoton* is *hear ye, hearing: i.e.,* give diligent heed, or hear patiently. Compare Isa. vi. 9.

[5] Job's discourse now changes from the third person (pl.) to the second (sing.) marking his appeal to God.

[6] The one challenged is first spoken of before he is directly addressed. In the next line Job seems to shrink back from his challenge, and yet feels he must go on to utter it, or die.

[7] It reads as if Job waited to see what the alternative was to be ; and finding it was the former, he proceeds.

25. Wilt Thou pursue me as a driven leaf?
    And chase me as the stubble [light and] dry?
26. For bitter things, against me, Thou dost write,
    And dost entail [1] on me my sins of youth.[2]
27. My feet Thou settest fast within the stocks,
    And lookest closely into all my ways,
    Making Thy mark upon my very feet.[3]
28. While these,[4] thus marked, in rottenness wear out,
    As garment when the moth hath eaten it.

—————[5]

xiv. 1. [Frail son of man] [6] that is of woman born,
    How few his days; and these, of trouble full!
2. He comes forth like a flow'r, and is cut down:
    He fleeth as a shadow; makes no stay.
3. Yet, op'nest Thou Thine eyes [7] on such an one,
    And him,[8] bring into judgment with Thyself?
4. Oh that a clean thing could come forth from out
    An unclean thing! But there is no such one.
5. If now his days are all [by Thee] decreed,
    And fixed the number of his months with Thee;
    If Thou hast made his bounds [9] he cannot pass;
6. Then look away from him that he may rest,
    And, like a hireling, may enjoy his day.

---

[1] Heb., *make me to inherit.*

[2] Heb., *the sins of my youth.*

[3] **As** owners of cattle and camels, **etc.,** put their mark upon the hoof, so that it may be known and traced. In *Kal,* it means *to mark,* but in *Hithpael* it means *to make thy mark for thyself.*

[4] **Heb.,** *it (i.e.,* each of my feet) **wears** out; or, *he* the person thus **marked** and watched.

[5] **Another brief pause.**

[6] Heb., אָדָם (*ādām*) *man* as distinguished from woman (Lat., *homo*).

[7] Textus Rec. *eye.* But eight early printed editions (one quoting from the Massorah) read *eyes* (pl.). See Ginsburg's Text and note.

[8] So it should be, with Sept., Syr. and Vulgate. See Ginsburg's Text and note.

[9] See Ginsburg's Heb. Text and note, that four early printed editions read the plural.

7. For of a tree, indeed, there still is hope
   That, if it be cut down, 'twill sprout again,
   And that its suckers will not cease [to grow].
8. Though, in the earth, the root thereof wax old,
   Though in the dust [of earth] its stump should die;
9. [Yet] will the waters' moistness¹ make it bud,
   And put forth shoots like newly-planted tree.
10. But man ²—he dies; and, fallèn, he departs:
    Yea, man—when he expireth—Where [is he]?
11. As waters fail, and vanish from the sea,
    And as a river wasteth and dries up;
12. So man lies down and riseth not again:
    Until the heavens are no more³ they ne'er
    Awake; nor are aroused from their sleep.
    ————— 4

13. Oh! that in Sheol Thou wouldst cover me;
    Conceal me, till Thine anger turn away,
    Fix me a time; and then remember me.
    ————— 4

14. If a man dies, Will he not live again? ⁵
    Then—all the days appointed I will wait,
    Until the time of my reviving ⁶ come;
15. Then shalt Thou call, and I will answer Thee;
    For Thou wilt yearn ⁷ toward Thy handwork.
    ——— 8

16. But now—Thou numberest my ev'ry step:
    And thou wilt not pass over ⁹ [all] my sin

---

¹ Heb., רִיחַ (*reyach*) *odour*, from root *to smell* or *drawing in* by inhalation. So fire can be drawn in (Judg. xvi. 9); also *odour*. Gen. viii. 21.

² Heb., גֶּבֶר (*gever*) *the strong man*. See note on ch. iv. 17.

³ See the Idiom in Ps. lxxii. 7. A.V. "So long as the moon endureth." Marg., "Heb., *till there be no moon.*"

⁴ A brief pause and change of thought.

⁵ Quite as exclamatory as interrogatory.

⁶ The Heb., חָלַף (*chalaph*), referring to the *regermination* of the tree in verse 7.

⁷ Compare Ps. civ. 31; cxxxviii. 8.

⁸ A pause is to be made here.

⁹ So it should be, according to Septuagint. See note Ginsburg's Heb. Text.

17. For, sealèd is my guilt, as in a bag,
   And mine iniquity Thou fast'nest up.

————— 1

18. Yes !—e'en a mountain falling, wastes away ;
   The rock may be removèd from its place ;
19. The [flowing] water wear away the stones ;
   The floods thereof may wash away the soil :
   E'en so the frail man's [2] hope Thou dost destroy.
20. Thou overpow'rest him, and he is gone ;
   His face doth fade ; Thou sendest him away.
21. His sons are honoured, but he knows it not ;
   They are brought low, but he perceives it not.
22. Only [till then] [3] he [4] pain feels over it,
   Only [till then] he [5] mourneth over it.[6]

---

[1] A slight pause here.

[2] See note on ch. iv. 17.

[3] *i.e.*, in prospect of all this ; till all this evil comes upon the man.

[4] Heb., *his flesh: i.e.*, by *Synecdoche* for *himself.*

[5] Heb., *his soul: i.e.*, by *Synecdoche* for *himself* The figure is used here to mark the fact that the one is outward and the other inward ; that it is the body that feels the pain, and the man himself that mourns.

[6] We have a similar construction in Hos. x. 5.

" The people thereof shall *mourn over it,*
And the priests thereof that *rejoiced over it* [shall mourn]."

The Hebrew is יָלָיו (*ālāiv*) *over it.* Not necessarily " over him." Rotherham so translates Hos. x. 5, and Young renders it " on account of it." This is its meaning here. It seems very strained to take the same word in one line "upon," and in the next line "within" as A.V. and R.V.

ELIPHAZ. SECOND ADDRESS.

k⁴. (page 63) chap. **xv.**

k⁴. | F | **xv.** 1-16.   On Job's reasonings.
G | **xv.** 17-35.   On God's dealings.

———————————

F. (above) **xv.** 1-16.   *On Job's reasonings.*

F | a | **xv.** 1-3.   Questions concerning Job's words.
b | 4-6.   Proofs in answer.
a | 7-14.   Questions concerning Job's character.
b | 15, 16.   Proofs in answer.

———————————

G. (above) **xv.** 17-35.   *On God's dealings.*

G | c | **xv.** 17-24.   God's judgments.
d | 25-27.   Reasons. The procuring cause.
c | 28-34.   God's judgments.
d | 35.   Reasons. The procuring cause.

a. (page 102), chap. xv. 1-3. *Questions concerning Job's words.*

xv. 1. Then answered ELIPHAZ the Temanite and said :
  2. A wise man, should he utter empty words ? [1]
   Or fill himself [2] with words like blustering wind ?
  3. Should he contend with words of no avail,
   Or speeches wherewith he can do no good ?

  b. (page 102), ch. xv. 4-6. *Proofs in answer.*

  4. But thou—thou wouldst make void the fear of God, [3]
   And weaken [all] devotion [due] to Him.
  5. Thy mouth declares thine own iniquity ;
   And thou thyself dost choose the crafty tongue.
  6. Thine own mouth doth condemn thee ; and not I ;
   Yea, thine own lips, against thee, testify.

a. (page 102), ch. xv. 7-14. *Questions concerning Job's character.*

  7. Art thou the first man who was [ever] born ?
   Wast thou brought forth before the hills [were made] ?
  8. Eloah's secret counsel didst thou hear ?
   And to [His] wisdom canst thyself attain ? [4]
  9. What knowest thou, that is not known to us ?
   What understandest thou, that we do not ?
  10. (The grey-haired and the aged are with us,
   More full of days than thine own father was.)
  11. God's comfortings, [5] Are they too small for thee ?

---

[1] Heb., *words or thoughts of wind.*
[2] Heb., *his breast* or *belly.* Put by Metonymy for *himself.* The two lines are synthetic. The first refers to what is *useless,* the second to what is *mischievous.* The next two lines correspond with these two.
[3] Heb., *El.*
[4] So it should be, with Septuagint. See Ginsburg's Heb. Text and note.
[5] Or, *our strong comfortings.* Heb. *comfortings* or *consolations of El.* By *Enallage* the Divine names are used in regimen as adjectives denoting that which is great, high, mighty. glorious, beautiful, or strong. Compare "wrestlings of God" (Gen. xxx, 8). "Voices of God" (Ex. ix. 28). "A trespass of Jehovah" (2 Chron. xxviii. 13, *i.e.,* a terrible sin). "A blast of Eloah" (Job iv. 9, *i.e.,* a vehement blast). "Cedars of God" (Ps. lxxx. 10). "Mountains of God" (Ps. xxxvi. 6). "Trees of the Lord" (Ps. civ. 16), &c. (See *Figures of Speech,* by the same author and publisher, pp. 502, 3).

Or is there any secret[1] [sin] with thee?
12. Why let thy feelings carry thee away?
    What meaneth, then, this quiv'ring of thine eyes?
13. That thou shouldst turn thy rage against [thy] GOD,[2]
    And cause such words to issue from thy mouth.
14. What is a mortal that he should be pure?
    Or, he of woman born, that he be just?

b. (page 102) chap. xv. 15, 16. *Proofs in Answer.*

15. Lo! in His holy ones He trusteth not;
    The very heavn's in His sight are not pure.
16. How much less [man], corrupt, defiled! Yea, man,
    Who drinks, like water [his] iniquity.

c. (page 102) chap. xv. 17-24. *God's Judgments.*

17. Give heed to me; and thee I will instruct;
    And that which I have seen I will declare:
18. (Which wise men plainly have made known to us,
    And have not hid them—truths their fathers taught;
19. The men to whom alone their land was given,
    And among whom no alien passed):[3]   [They said]
20.   'The wicked sorely labours all his days,
      'His years[4] reserved[5] for the oppressor's greed.
21.   'A voice of terror[6] ever fills his ears;
      'And when he prospers, then the spoiler comes.'
22.   'He has no hope[7] from darkness to return,
      '[And thinks][8] that he is destined for the sword;[9]

---

1 From לָהַט (*lahat*) *to muffle up.*
Not the same word as in verse 8.
There it was סוֹד (*sūd*) a secret,
answering to the Greek μυστήριον
(*musterion*) *mystery*, or the Divine
secret purpose or counsel.

2 Heb. *El.*

3 *i.e.*, they were undisturbed by
invasion and had leisure to think.

4 Heb., *the number of his years.*

5 Heb., *laid up.*

6 Heb., *terrors.*

7 Heb., *he believeth not;* i.e., he
despairs.

8 A verb must be supplied here to
correspond with the previous line.

9 Sept., *the power of the sword.*

23.   ' He wanders forth and asks :—O, where is bread,
        ' Well knowing that a dark day [1] draweth nigh.
24.   ' Distress and anguish fill him with alarm ;
        ' They overpow'r him like a warrior's charge.'

d. (page 102) chap. xv. 25-27. *Reasons. The procuring cause.*

25.   ' Because he stretchèd out his hand 'gainst GOD [2]
        ' And proudly did defy El Shaddai,
26.   ' [Because] he used to run with stiffened neck
        ' Against Him, with the bosses of his shield.
27.   ' Because his face he clothed with his own fat, [3]
        ' And gathered rolls of fat upon his loins.

c. (page 102) chap. xv. 28-34. *God's Judgments.*

28.   ' Therefore he dwelleth in a ruined place,
        ' In houses wherein no one else would live.
        ' In places destined to be ruined heaps.
29.   ' He'll not be rich, nor will his wealth endure ;
        ' Nor will his shadow [4] lengthen on the ground.
30.   ' From darkness he will nevermore escape ;
        ' His tender branch the flame shall wither up ;
        ' In God's [5] hot anger he will pass away.
31.   ' Let no one put his trust in vain deceit :
        ' For vanity will be his recompense ;
32.   ' [And] he will be cut off [6] before his time, [7]
        ' So that his palm [8] will not be always green. [9]
33.   ' As shaketh off, the vine, its unripe fruit,
        ' Or, as the olive casts away its flower.

---

[1] Heb., *a day of darkness.*
[2] Heb., *El.*
[3] Compare Ps. xvii. 10.
[4] So the Sept. See note in Ginsburg's Heb. Text.
[5] Heb., *His, i.e.,* not the man's own, but God's hot anger. Compare ch. iv. 9.

[6] So A.V. margin.
[7] Heb., בְּלֹא יוֹמוֹ (*belo yōmŏ*) *not yet his day, i.e.,* prematurely.
[8] *Or his palm branch* or *top,* as in Isa. ix. 13 ; xix. 15.
[9] *i.e.,* will not flourish, but wither away.

34.   ' So will the household of the vile be naught,
        ' And fire consume the tents of the corrupt.[1]

d. (page 102) chap. xv. 35. *Reasons. The procuring cause.*

35.   ' For evil they conceive,[2] and mischief bear,
        ' Their heart doth travail with iniquity.[3]

---

[1] Heb., *of bribery.*

[2] The two verbs are in the Infinitive. But by the figure *Heterosis*, the Indicative gives the sense. See Gen. viii. 5 ; Ex. viii. 15 ; 2 Sam. iii. 18 ; 1 Kings xxii. 30 ; 2 Ch. xviii. 29 ; xxxi. 10 ; Ps. viii. 1 ; xxxii. 9, lxxvii. 1 ; Prov. xii. 6 ; Isa. v. 5 ; xxxviii.16 ; xlix. 7 ; Jer. vii. 9 ; xiv. 5 ; Ezek. i. 14 ; xi. 7 ; Hab. ii. 15 ; and see *Figures of Speech*, pp. 510-516.

[3] Compare Ps. vii. 14 :—

    "Behold he travaileth with
        iniquity ;
    Yea, he hath conceived mis-
        chief
    And brought forth iniquity."

This is, at the root, the procuring cause of all the judgments of God.

JOB'S SECOND REPLY TO ELIPHAZ.

1⁴. (page 63) chaps. xvi., xvii

H 1. (above) chap. xvi. 1-6. *Job's Reproof.*

xvi. 1. Then did Job answer [Eliphaz] and say :—
2. Of such like things I have abundance heard ;
[Yea] ministers of trouble[1] are ye all.
3. Shall such vain words[2] come never to an end ?
Or what emboldens thee to answer still ?
4. For I also could speak as well as you.
If YE were in distress instead of ME[3]
I could heap words together against you ;[4]
Against you I could shake my head in scorn.
5. With MY mouth I could [also] harden you,
And with my lip I, too, could you restrain.[5]
6. Though, if I speak, my grief is not assuaged ;[6]
If I forbear, how much of it departs ?[7]

---

[1] Heb., *ministers of trouble* and *distress.*

[2] Instead of ministering words of comfort, ministering only *words of wind.*

[3] Heb., If your person[s were] instead of my person.

[4] Heb., *I could join* [myself] *to you.* The verb being in the *Hiphil* denotes more than simply *joining* , it means *setting in array.*

[5] The primary meaning of חָשַׂךְ (*chasak*) is *to restrain, keep back.* See Gen. xx. 16 ; xxxix. 9, 2 Sam. xviii. 16 and especially Prov. x. 19. Hence *to darken* by restraining the light, ch. xviii. 6 ; xiii. 10 ; iii. 8. The ordinary rendering of this verse entirely misses the scope of the passage of which it forms part.

[6] The same word as in the previous line. But here in the *Niphal,* and is reflexive.

[7] Heb. *what goeth from me.*

I[1]. (page 107) chap. xvi. 7-16. *Job's Despondency.*

7. Ah! God[1] hath verily exhausted me![2]
   Yea all my family Thou hast destroyed.

8. And shrivelled up my skin. Look! what a sight!
   My leanness like a witness riseth up
   And testifies my ruin to my face.

   ——————— [3]

9. His[8] anger rends, and maketh war on me,
   And He hath gnashed upon me with His teeth. [4]
   He is mine enemy; His eyes are swords;[5]

10. [And vile] men gape upon me with their mouths;[6]
    And, with contempt, they smite me on my cheeks,
    And band themselves together against me.

11. God, to the evil one delivers me,
    And headlong casts me to malignant hands.

12 At ease, I was, when He did shatter me;
    He seized my neck, and dashed me to the ground:
    Then picked me up, and set me for His mark.

13. His archers did encompass me around.
    One cleaves my reins asunder—spares me not;
    Another pours my gall upon the earth;

14. Another breaketh me with breach on breach;
    He runneth at me like a man of war.

15. I have sewn sackcloth round about myself. [7]
    My glory[8] is defilèd in the dust.

16. My face with weeping has become inflamed,[9]
    And o'er mine eyelids comes the shade of death.

---

[1] Heb., *He.* The change of pronoun in the next line intensifies the pathos.

[2] The desolation referred to in the next line, by the loss of his children, demands a stronger word than "weary" in this line.

[3] A slight pause here.

[4] Compare Ps. xxxv. 16; xxxvii. 12, &c.

[5] Heb., *whetteth* or *sharpeneth His eyes against,* as we speak of *looking daggers* at one.

[6] Compare Ps. xxii. 13.

[7] Heb., *my skin*: put, by *Synecdoche,* for the whole person.

[9] Heb., *my horn*: put, by *Metonymy,* for *my glory,* or *pride.*

[8] Heb., *red.*

H². (page 107) chap. xvi. 17-21. *Job's Reply.*

17. [All this] was not for wrong that I had done; [1]
    My prayer was pure [made in sincerity]
18. (O Earth! do not thou cover up my blood;
    And let my cry [for vengeance] have no rest.)
19. E'en now, Lo! in the heav'ns, my witness is,
    And He who voucheth for me is on high. [2]
20. My friends are they who scorn me, [mock my grief].
    But to Eloah, I [3] pour out my tears,
21. That He might justify me with Himself,
    E'en as a son of man pleads for his friend.

I². (page 107) chap. xvi. 22-xvii. 1. *Job's Despondency.*

22. For yet a few more years will come and go,
    And I shall be whence I shall not return.
xvii. 1. My heart [4] is broken; [and] my days are quench'd.
    Graves shall I seek and [yet I shall] not find. [5]

H³. (page 107) chap. xvii. 2-10. *Job's Challenge.*

2. Surely [6] do those who mock, beset me round,
   Mine eye doth on their provocation rest.
3. Give me a pledge, [7] I pray; be Thou my bond; [8]
   Who is there [else] will pledge himself for me? [9]
4. [Not they]. [10] THEIR heart, from wisdom, Thou hast **hid**:
   Thou wilt not then let them prevail. [It's said] [11]

---

[1] Compare the similar construction in Isa. liii. 9. Lit., *was in my hand.*

[2] Heb., *in the heights above.*

[3] Heb., *mine eye;* put, by *Synecdoche* for *myself.*

[4] Heb., *my spirit.*

[5] So the Sept. See note Ginsburg's Heb. Text.

[6] Heb., אִם־לֹא *(im lo)* as in ch. i. 11; xxii. 20; xxxi. 36, &c., as a form of asseveration.

[7] So R.V. Or, *arrange* it thus.

[8] Compare the same **word in** Isa. xxviii. 14.

[9] Heb., *to strike hands*, is the **Idiom** (arising from *Mentonymy of the Adjunct)* for pledging one's self, **or** concluding a bargain. See *Figures of Speech,* pp. 607, 857.

[10] *i.e.,* not my friends.

[11] It seems as if Job is here quoting a well-known saying.

5. ' When one for profit [1] doth betray his friends;
   ' His very children look to him in vain.' [2]
6. But me HE's made a byword to the world :
   I am become an object of contempt.[3]

——————— [4]

7. Therefore mine eye becometh dim from grief ;
   And all my limbs [5] are to a shadow shrunk.
8. The upright will astounded be at this,
   The pure be stirr'd by [treatment so] unjust.
9. But still the righteous will hold on his way ;
   The innocent [6] will go from strength to strength.
10. [Despite] them [7] all, come now, I beg of you ;
    Shall I not find among you one wise man ?

I [3]. (page 107) chap. xvii. 11-16. *Job's Despondency.*[8]

11. My days are passed ; [and all] my purposes
    Are broken off ; [9]—my heart's most cherished [10] plans.
12. Night is [11] appointed me instead of day :
    [My] light is drawing near to darkness [deep].

---

[1] Heb., *a share of booty ;* or *spoil.*
[2] Heb., *shall fail,* or *be consumed* (*i.e.,* with longing), and be disappointed. Compare ch. xxxi. 16. Ps. lxix. 3.
[3] Heb., *spitting,* which is an idiomatic expression for showing contempt.
[4] A slight pause for change of thought.
[5] Or, My shapely limbs are to a shadow shrunk.
[6] Heb., *clean of hands* (*i.e.,* Job himself). The four lines of verses 8 and 9, are an alternate parallel :—

a | 8-. Righteous. ⎫ Others.
b | -8. Innocent. ⎭
a | 9-. Righteous. ⎫ Job
b | -9. Innocent. ⎭ himself.

In verse 8 it is general. In verse 9 it is particular, and Job alludes to himself.
[7] Some codices with Syr. and Vulg. read "you." The A.V. and R.V. apparently followed the Vulgate. See Ginsburg's Text and note.
[8] Corresponding with I[2] (xvi. 22 —xvii. 1).
[9] The expression refers to a weaver's loom. Compare Isa. xxxviii. 12.
[10] Heb., *possessions,* or *treasures.*
[11] Heb., *they appoint*: "they"; not the friends but his calamities. He has turned from his friends, and in this member is occupied with himself.

13. If I should hope, Lo, Sheol is my home ;
    Yea in the darkness I should make my bed ;
14. ' My Father thou '—I say now to the grave ; [1]
    ' My Mother ' and ' my Sister '—to the worm.
15. [' If I should hope,' I said ;] where then is it ?
    And who [alas !] should see my blessedness ? [2]
16. With me [2] to Sheol would they both go down,
    And rest together, with me, in the dust.[3]

---

[1] Heb., שַׁחַת (*shachath*) is not generally taken as *corruption* though other
passages support this interpretation.
It is from שׁוּחַ (*shuch*), *to dig*, not from
שָׁחַת (*shackhath*) *to corrupt*. The Sept.
and Vulg. render it *death*.
 [2] So it should be with **Septuagint**.
See Ginsburg's Text and note.
 [3] As in ch. vii. 22.

BILDAD'S SECOND ADDRESS.

k⁵. (page 63) chap. xviii.

k⁵ | J | 1-4. Reproof of Job.
   | K | 5-21. Doom of the wicked.

Expansion of K. (above) ch. xviii. 5-21. *Doom of the wicked.*

K | L | 5-20. Particular.
  | M | 21. General.

Expansion of L. (above) xviii. 5-20. *Particular.*

L | e | 5, 6. Extinction.

   f | 7-16. Evils { *vv.* 7, 8, from the man himself.
                         { *vv.* 9-16, from others.

  e | 17-19. Extinction.

   f | 20. Astonishment of others.

J. (above) xviii. 1-4. *Bildad's reproof of Job.*

1. Then BILDAD, the Shuite, spoke a second time,[1] and said :—
2. How long will ye[2] thus hunt about for words ?[3]
   Pray understand, and after, let us speak.
3. Wherefore are we accounted like the beasts,
   [And wherefore] held as worthless[4] in thine[5] eyes ?
4. Lo ! in his anger 'tis himself[6] he rends,
   For thee, shall Earth be rendered desolate ?
   Or, shall the rock be movèd from its place ?

---

[1] See note on ch. iii. 2.

[2] Bildad again addresses Job in the plural (ch. viii. 2) probably speaking to him as representing a class: as Job had done before in his reply to Zophar (ch. xii. 2). All spoke at greater length than Bildad, and so he may be speaking to all the parties, and not merely Job.

[3] Heb., *huntings of words.*

[4] The Heb. is written as meaning *stupid*, but it is to be read *unclean*. Our rendering *worthless* expresses both ideas.

[5] So it should be with Sept. and Syr. See Ginsburg's Heb. text and note : referring to Job.

[6] Heb., *his own soul.* In ch. xvi. 9 Job had said·it was God who thus dealt with him.

L. (page 112) chap. xviii. 5-20. *Doom of the wicked.* (*Particular.*)

e. (page 112) chap. xviii. 5, 6. *Extinction.*

5. Yes! True! the sinner's light shall be put out,
And from his fire no bright flame shall ascend.
6. Daylight, shall[1] darkness in his tent become,
The lamp which hangs above him[2] shall go out.

f. (page 112) chap. xviii. 7-16. *Evils of the wicked.*

7. His once firm step[3] shall [halt], and weakened be,
And his own counsel cast him headlong down.
8. By his own feet he's urged into a net,
For in his chosen way[4] there lies a snare.
9. The [hidden] snare shall seize him by the heel;
The noose shall [catch him and shall] hold him fast.—
10. The snare lies hidden for him in the ground;
The trap in ambush waits beside his path,
11. Terrors shall startle him on every side;
[At every step] they make his feet to start.
12. His woe[5] doth hunger for him [as its prey]:
A dire disease stands ready at his side.
13. The members of his body to consume;
Yea, Death's First-born,[6] his members shall devour,
14. Uproot him from his tent (in which he trusts),
And to the King of Terrors,[7] hurry him.

---

[1] Heb., *has become dark.* It is the perfect tense, implying certainty, and may well be rendered by the future.
[2] Or, *beside.*
[3] Heb., *the steps of his strength.*
[4] The *Hithpael* quite justifies this rendering.
[5] The Heb. is not אוֹן (*ōn*) *strength* (as Vulg. followed by A.V. and R.V.) but the *construct* of אָוֶן (*aven*) *calamity, woe*: Woe being put, by *Metonymy*, for the calamity which causes it.
[6] Some malignant disease is expressed by this *Figure* (*Periphrasis*).
[7] Death is personified by this *Periphrasis.*

15. Strange creatures[1] in his habitation dwell:
Brimstone [from heaven][2] is rained down o'er his home.[3]

16. [While], from beneath, his roots shall be dried up,
And from above, his branch shall be cut off.

e. (page 112) chap. xviii. 17-19. *Extinction.*

17. His memory has perish'd from the Earth,
No name is left to him in all the land.[4]

18. From light to darkness do they[5] thrust him forth,
And from the world he's driven[5] far away.[6]

19. Childless[7] among his people he is left,
In all his habitation none survive.

f. (page 112) chap. xviii. 20. *Astonishment of others.*

20. Those who come after, wonder at his doom,[8]
As those who went before were seized with fear.

M. (page 112) chap. xviii. 21. *The doom of the wicked. (General.)*

21. Such, are the dwellings of [all] wicked men ;
Yea, such the place of him who knows not GOD.[9]

---

[1] Heb., *it: i.e.*, every one of them, and so may be rendered by the plural. Or, it may be taken as Impersonal— *There shall dwell.* These dwellers are not strange men. The Heb. is *none of his: i.e.*, *strange beings* such as those mentioned in Is. xiii. 20, &c. ; xxvii. 10, &c. ; xxxiv. 11, &c. ; Zeph. ii. 9. Such as these dwell in his ruined home, made desolate by the brimstone rain from heaven.

[2] As in Gen. xix. 24. Ps. xi. 6.

[3] Heb., נָוֵהוּ (*nâhvehū*) his *pleasant place*, or *home*.

[4] In the first line אֶרֶץ (*eretz*) is *the earth* ; while in the second line חוּץ (*chūtz*) is the open field or *plain* (more local).

[5] See note on ch. vii. 3.

[6] Heb., *do they drive.* Compare Ps. xlix. 15. Prov. xiv. 32, "The arched man is *driven away* in his wickedness.

[7] Heb., *no sprout, no shoot.* But this would be too literal. *No chick nor child* would preserve the alliteration נִין וְנֶכֶד *Nin and Neked* ; but would not be less poetic, than " son nor nephew" of the A.V. ; or " son nor grandson" of the R.V.

[8] Heb., *day*, put by *Metonymy* (of Adjunct) for what happens in the day : *i.e.*, here judgment. Compare 1 Cor. iv. 2, and Rev. i. 10. Where " Man's day" and "The Lord's day " mean the day when they judge and will judge, respectively.

[9] Heb., *El.*

JOB'S REPLY TO BILDAD'S SECOND ADDRESS.

1⁵. (page 63) chap. xix.

1⁵| N | xix. 1-5.   Censure of his friends for their reproaches.

O | 6-20.   Complaints to them of God's dealings as his enemy.

O | 21-27.   Appeal to them of his hope in God his Redeemer.

| N | 28, 29.   Warning to his friends, to cease their reproaches.

N. (above) chap. xix. 1-5.   *Censure of his friends for their reproaches.*

1. Then JOB answered [Bildad], and said :—
2. How long will ye [thus grieve and] vex my soul?
   And break me all to pieces with your words?
3. Already,[1] ten times, me ye have reproach'd ;
   And yet are not ashamed to wrong[2] me[2] thus.
4. Be it that I have sinnèd, [as ye say],
   My sin is with myself [and God] alone.
5. If 'gainst me still ye magnify yourselves,
   And plead against me that I must have sinned :

O. (above) chap. xix. 6-20.   *Complaints to them of God's dealings as his enemy.*

6. Then know that Eloah hath overthrown
   My cause ; and made His net to close me round.

---

[1] Heb., *this : i.e.*, these ten times.
[2] So it should be, with Sept.   See Ginsburg's Text and note.

7. Behold, I cry out 'Wrong!' but am not heard:
   I cry out 'Help!' but there is no redress.

8. My path He hedgeth up;[1] I cannot pass;
   And on my way He hath made darkness rest.[2]

9. My glory, from me, He hath strippèd off,
   And from my head He hath remov'd the crown.[3]

10. On all sides I am crush'd,[4] where'er I go:
    He[5] hath my hope uprooted, like a tree.

11. Against me He hath made His anger burn,
    And counts me toward Him as His enemy.

12. Together ['gainst me] do His troops come on;
    Against me, they, their earthworks[6] have cast up,
    And round about my tent they have encamped.

13. My brethren hath He put far off[7] from me,
    And mine acquaintance[8] from me are estranged.

14. My near-of-kin[9] have ceased [and failèd] me,
    And my familiar friends[10] forgotten me,

15. The dwellers in my house, and maidens [too],
    Account [and treat] me as a stranger now:
    I am become an alien in their[11] eyes.

16. I called my servant,—but he answered not,
    [Though] I entreated him with mine own mouth.

17. My manner[12] seemeth strange unto my wife,
    My feelings[13] to the children that she bare.

---

1 Heb. נָדַר (*gadud*) *to fence up.*
Lam. iii. 7, 9. Hos. ii. 8 (6).

2 Compare ch. iii. 23 ; xiii. 27.

3 See the same collocation in Isa. lxi. 10.

4 Heb., *He hath crushed me.*

5 Heb., *and.*

6 Heb , *cast up their way*, or *mound*, which in war (the *Simile* here) is an earthwork, not a way.

7 Heb., *from near*, or *beside me.*

8 Heb., *they that know me*

9 Ps. xxxviii. 11 (12).

10 Ps. xxxi. 11 ; lxxxviii. 8.

11 A special class of various readings called *Severin*, read *your*. See Ginsburg's Heb. Text and note ; also his *Introduction* chap. iii. According to this reading Job is turning to them and addressing them personally in the three lines of this verse.

12 Heb., *spirit ;* here denoting, not breath, but *manner*, or *temper.* "Breath" can hardly be called "strange."

13 Heb., *the marks of my affection.*

18. Yea—e'en the very boys despise me now ;
    They jeer at me when I attempt [1] to rise.
19. My confidential friends [2] from me recoil :
    And those I loved turn right away from me. [3]
20. My bone cleaves fast unto my skin and flesh, [4]
    All shrunk away the cov'ring of my teeth. [5]

O. (page 115) chap. xix. 21-27. *Appeal to them of his hope in God,*
his Redeemer.

21. Have pity ; oh, have pity, ye, my friends ;
    Eloah's hand [alas !] hath stricken me. [6]
22. Wherefore pursue me as if ye were GOD ? [7]
    Will not my body's [ills] suffice for you ? [8]

———— [9]

23. Oh, that my words could now be written down !
    Oh, that a record could be graved [10] with pen
24. Of iron, cut in rock [and filled] with lead,
    A witness evermore. [The words are these].
25. I KNOW THAT MY REDEEMER EVER LIVES,
    AND AT THE LATTER DAY ON EARTH SHALL STAND ;
26. AND AFTER THEY [11] CONSUME MY SKIN, [EV'N] THIS—
    YET IN MY FLESH I SHALL ELOAH SEE :

---

[1] Heb., *The paragogic* ה *(he)* gives the subjunctive or optative sense.

[2] Heb., *the men of my counsel : i.e.,* those with whom Job was wont to consult.

[3] Or, *are turned against the sight,* as depicted in the next verse.

[4] *i.e.,* the bones nearly pierce and show through the skin, appearing to cleave to the skin.

[5] *i.e., the gums,* which shrink away and let the teeth escape. The Heb., verb, מָלַט *(malat)* means *to be smooth,* then *to slip away* (hence, to escape).

[6] Heb., *touched ; i.e.,* by the Figure,

Tapeinosis, smitten. See Ps. cxliv. 5.

[7] Heb., *El.*

[8] Heb., *Why, with my flesh be not content ?* Here, the flesh, is put for the body as that which suffers pain. Job asks, Why not be satisfied with my bodily sufferings, without adding the mental torture of your remorseless words.

[9] A slight pause to be made here.

[10] Heb., *could be inscribed in a book.*

[11] See note on ch. vii. 3. Here the "ptomaines" or worms, which after death consume the flesh and return it to dust.

27. W<small>HOM</small> I, <small>EV'N</small> I, <small>SHALL SEE UPON MY SIDE.</small>
     M<small>INE EYES SHALL SEE</small> H<small>IM—STRANGER, NOW, NO MORE.</small>
     [F<small>OR THIS</small>] <small>MY INMOST SOUL WITH LONGING WAITS.</small>

N. (page 115) ch. xix. 28, 29.   *Warning to his friends, to
                          cease their complaints.*

28. Ye shall [then] say,
                    ' Why did we him pursue ?
       ' Why seek to find in him [1] a root of blame ?' [2]
29. Beware ! and of the sword be ye afraid :
     For wrathful are the sword's dread punishments, [3]
     And ye shall know indeed its judgment [sure].

---

[1] So the Sept., Aramaic, Vulgate, and some Codices. See Ginsburg's Text and note.

[2] The A.V. and R.V. *matter* has little meaning, and takes it quite away from the scope of these two verses. It is rather the root, or the cause of all Job's trouble, which they were seeking to find out.

[3] Heb., *sins of the sword*, sins being put by *Metonymy* (of the cause) for that which calls for the punishment of the sword.

ZOPHAR'S SECOND ADDRESS.

k⁶. (page 63) chap. xx.

k⁶ | P | 1-5. His theme stated.

    Q | 6-28. Expansion of the theme.

  P | 29. The theme re-stated.

P. (above) xx. 1-5. *Zophar's theme stated.*

1. Then ZOPHAR, the Naamathite, spoke a second time,[1]
   and said
2. Not so : [2] my thoughts impel me to respond,
   And therefore is my haste within me [roused].
3. Chastisement meant for my reproof,[3] I hear,
   But zeal,[4] with knowledge, gives me a reply.
4. Know'st thou [not] this ?—a truth of olden time,
   Since Adam first was placed upon the earth ?
5. That brief the triumph of the wicked is,
   And momentary is the sinners' joy.

Q. (above) xx. 6-28. *Expansion of the theme.*

6. His joy may mount up to the [very] heav'ns,
   His head reach up unto the [highest] clouds.
7. Like his own stubble [5] he is swept away ;
   And they who saw, shall say, ' Where has he gone ? '

---

[1] See note on ch. iii. 2.

[2] So it should be, with Sept. See Ginsburg's text and note.

[3] Like Isa. liii. 5, *chastisement of our peace ; i.e.,* meant for, or which tends to our peace.

[4] Heb. רוּחַ (*ruach*) *spirit.* Here it may well be rendered *zeal ; i.e., warmth of feeling.*

[5] So it should be, with Septuagint. See Ginsburg's Heb. Text and note.

8. He fleeth as a dream, and is not found :
   He's chased away like visions of the night.
9. The eye which saw him seeth him not again ;
   His dwelling-place beholdeth him no more.
10. His children shall pay court unto [1] the poor ;
    And his own hands give back again his wealth.[2]
11. His bones are filled with sins [3] in secret [4] done,
    And with him in the dust they [5] shall lie down.
12. Though wickedness, while in his mouth, be sweet,
    Though underneath his tongue he keeps it hid,—
13. Keeping [6] it long, and loth to let it go,
    Retaining it within his palate's taste ; [7]
14. Yet, in his bowels, is his food [8] all changed ;
    Within him it becomes the gall of asps.
15. He swallowed wealth, but vomiteth it up :
    Yea from his belly GOD [9] will drive it forth.
16. The venom of the adder shall he suck ;
    The poison [10] of the viper slayeth him.
17. He shall not look upon the [flowing] streams,
    Or floods, or brooks of honey and of milk.
18. In vain [11] he toiled, he shall not swallow [it] ;
    Like wealth giv'n back, in it he has no joy.
19. Because he crush'd, and helpless left the poor ;
    [And] seized upon a house he did not build.

---

[1] Heb., *conciliate, appease*, or *seek the favour* of the poor.

[2] *i.e.*, by means of his children, who have to use it to propitiate even the poor.

[3] *Sins*, put by *Metonymy* for the results of sin which are experienced in his bones, which go down with a man to his grave,

[4] Lit., *secret things*.

[5] Heb., *fem sing*, used collectively.

[6] Heb., *sparing it*.

[7] In these four lines the figure *Synonymia* emphasises the persistency with which the sinner pursues his lustful enjoyment, which is compared to a dainty morsel in the mouth.

[8] Heb., *meat* put by *Synecdoche* for *food*.

[9] Heb., *El*.

[10] Heb , tongue, put by *Metonymy* (of the Adjunct) for the *poison* contained in it.

[11] So it should be, with Sept. See Ginsburg's Text and note.

20. Because content, within, he never knew,
    Nor let escape him ought that he desired.
21. (No, not a shred that he devourèd not),
    Therefore it is, his wealth [1] shall not endure.
22. When wealth is at its height, his straits begin,
    The power of distress [2] shall come on him.
23. For when he is about to eat his food,
    Then [God] shall send on him His burning wrath
    And rain it on him for his punishment [3]
24. [Though] he may flee away from lance of iron,
    The [arrow from] the bow of brass shall pierce him through :
25. [And if] one draws it forth from out his flesh,
    The gleaming arrow-head from out his gall,
    [Then other] terrors shall upon him come.
26. For his hid-treasures every trouble [4] waits ;
    A fire not blown [by man] [5] devours them all ;
    It shall consume what in his tent is left.
27. The heav'ns shall his iniquity reveal.
    Against him riseth up the [very] earth,
28. The increase of his house to exile goes,
    Like flowing waters, in God's [6] day of wrath.

P. (page 119) chap. xx. 29. *The theme re-stated.*

29. Such is the sinner's portion sent from God ; [7]
    And such the doom GOD [8] hath appointed him.

---

[1] In the old English sense of the word. Not riches merely, but his *weal* or *good*.

[2] So it should be, with Sept. and Vulgate. See Ginsburg's text and note.

[3] So Fuerst's Lexicon. "With his food" (Tregelles's Gesenius). "Into his very bowels" (Oxford Gesenius 536a).

[4] Heb., *darkness*, put by *Metonymy* for *calamity*.

[5] "But kindled from heaven" (Oxford Gesenius, 518 b, 1 c. Compare 656 a).

[6] Heb., *His*.

[7] Heb., *Elohim*.

[8] Heb., *El*.

JOB'S REPLY TO ZOPHAR'S SECOND ADDRESS.

1⁶. (page 63) chap. xxi.

1⁶ | R¹ | 1-6.   Appeal to his friends.

   S | 7-26.   Contrasted cases.   The wicked (7-21)
     | The good (22-26.) *

   R² | 27-29.   Appeal to his friends.

   S | 30-33.   Contrasted case.   The wicked in life
     | (30, 31).   In death (32, 33).*

   R³ | 34.   Appeal to his friends.

---

* Expansion of S and *S* (above) chap. xxi. 7-26 and 30-33.

S | g¹ | 7-16.   Prosperity.   ⎫
  | h¹ | 17-21.   Adversity.   ⎬ The wicked.
  | g² | 22-24.   Prosperity.   ⎫
  | h² | 25, 26.   Adversity.   ⎬ The good.

S | g³ | 30, 31.   Prosperity in life.   ⎫
    | h³ | 32, 33.   Prosperity in death.   ⎬ The wicked.

R¹. (page 122) chap. xxi. 1-6). *Job's appeal to his friends.*

1. Then JOB answered [Zophar's second address] and said.
2. Oh, listen patiently unto my words;
   And so let this your consolation be.
3. Oh, bear with me, I pray, and let me speak;
   And after I have spoken, thou¹ canst mock.
4. Ah me! Do I make my appeal to man?
   Might I not in that case impatient be?
5. Turn now, and look on me, and stand amazed,
   And lay ye now your hand upon your mouth.
6. For, when I think of it, I am dismayed,
   And trembling taketh hold upon my flesh.

S. (page 122) chap. xxi. 7-26. *Contrasted cases.*

g¹. (page 122) chap. xxi. 7-16. *Prosperity of the wicked.*

7. Why [suffers God] ungodly men to live,
   And to grow old, yea, to wax strong in power?
8. With them their seed's established; yea, with them
   Their offspring [live and] grow before their eyes.
9. Their houses are in peace; they know no fear;
   No scourge descends upon them from 𝕲𝕺𝕯'𝕾 ² hand.
10. Their bull engendereth, and doth not fail;
    Their cow doth calve, and casteth not her calf.
11. Their little children skip about like lambs;
    Their elder children³ mingle in the dance.

---

¹ In former addresses Job, though general, was also personal in his replies , *e.g.*, in xvi. 8, he singled out Eliphaz. In xxvi. 2-4 he singles out Bildad. So here, he singles out Zophar. It reminds us of the saying of Themistocles, "Strike, but hear me!" (Plutarch, Themist, c. 11).

² Heb., *Eloah.*

³ עֲוִילֵיהֶם (*avĭleyhem*) *elder children* is in contrast with the יַלְדֵיהֶם (*yaldeyhem*) *little ones* of the previous line.

12. With timbrel and with harp they left their voice ;
    And merry make with cheerful sound of pipe.
13. They, in prosperity, complete [1] their days,
    And in a moment to the grave [2] go down.
14. Yet, unto GOD [3] they say :

    'Depart from us ;
    ' No knowledge of THY ways do we desire.
15. ' Who is Shaddai that we should serve Him ?
    ' And what the profit if to Him we pray ?

    ——————— [4]

16. But lo ! their good comes not from their own hand.
    The ways [5] of wicked men are far from me.

h [1]. (page 122) chap. xxi. 17-21. *Adversity of the wicked.*

17.   [But yet, YE say]
    How oft goes out the lamp of evil men !
    [How oft] calamity on them doth come !
    [How oft] are pangs apportioned them in wrath !
18. [How oft] are they as straw before the blast,
    Like chaff the storm and tempest drive away !
19. [Ye say] Eloah treasures for [6] his sons
    His evil life, and it requites, that he

---

1 In the Heb. text it is written *wear out* or *consume* ; but it is read *complete* or *fill up*. Some Codices, with one early-printed edition, the Aramaic Sept., Syr., and Vulg. versions, both *read* and *write* it " complete." See Ginsburg's Heb. Text and note.

2 Heb., *Sheol.*

3 Heb., *El.*

4 A slight pause.

5 Heb., עֵץ (*yăatz*) *to deliberate.* Hence, *counsel,* implying both deliberation and the carrying of it out. The rendering " way " includes both, and the meaning is that the thoughts and acts of the wicked are past comprehension.

6 The rhythm precludes the possibility of expressing the fulness of the line in the original, which reads " Eloah treasures up his evil for his sons " : *i.e.,* the wicked man's sins are visited on his children. (At least this was what Job's friends said.) It is all implied in our word " visiteth."

20. May know ; and his own eyes [1] his trouble see,
When from the wrath of Shaddai he drinks.
21. What pleasure hath he in prosperity,
When cut off are the number of his months ?

g². (page 122) chap. xxi. 22-24. *Prosperity of the good.*

22. Is it to GOD [2] that one can knowledge teach ?
Seeing 'tis He who judgeth things on high !
23. [For, lo]: one dieth in the very height
Of his prosperity, calm, and at ease :
24. His breasts are full of nourishment ; his bones
With marrow are well moistenèd, [and fresh].

h². (page 122), chap. xxi. 25, 26. *Adversity of the good.*

25. Another dies in bitterness of soul,
And never had he tasted any good.
26. Together in the dust they both lie down,
Alike o'er both, the worm, its covering spreads.

R². (page 122) chap. xxi. 27-29. *Appeal to his friends.*

27. Behold, [my friends], I know your thoughts ; which ye
Against me do so wrongfully [3] maintain,
28. Ye say
‘ Where is the dwelling of the Prince ? [4]
‘ And where the tent wherein the wicked dwell ?

---

[1] The Heb. Text is *written* "eye," but is to be *read*, "eyes." But in some Codices, with two early printed editions, Aramaic, Syriac, Septuagint and Vulgate, "eyes" (plural) is both *written* and *read.*

[2] Heb., *El.*

[3] Heb , חָמָס (*chamas*) *injury*, **is** generally associated with *violence*, but here, the context requires the sense of injustice.

[4] Heb., *the noble-minded*, or **any** person of high degree.

29. Have ye not asked of Travellers?[1]   Do not
    Ignore[2] what they have noted down. [3]   [They say] :—

S. (page 122) chap. xxi. 30-33).   *Contrasted case.*

g.[3] (*vv.* 30, 31).   *Prosperity of the wicked in life.*

30.   ' The wicked, in the day of wrath,[4] is spared ; [5]
       ' Yea, in the day of wrath he doth escape.' [6]

31. Who, to his face, will dare denounce his way?
    Who shall requite him that which he hath done?

h [3]. (page 122) chap. xxi. 32, 33.   *Prosperity of the wicked at death.*

32. Yet, to the grave [6] he is in honour brought ;[7]
    And o'er his monument one keepeth watch.[8]

33. The valley's clods do gently [9] cover him,
    Behind, [the mourners] come in lengthened train ; [10]
    Before, they all in countless numbers walk.

R [3]. (page 122) chap. xxi. 34.   *Appeal to his friends.*

34. How then console ye me with worthless [11] [words]
    Seeing your answers, only failure, prove?

---

[1] Heb., *the passers by the way.* The Idiom for travellers.

[2] The *Piel* here expresses the negative of knowing ; *i.e.*, *to ignore, disregard.* Compare Deu. xxxii. 27 ; 1 Sam. xxiii. 7 ; Jer. xix. 4.

[3] Heb., *their signs ;* or marks made on standards, which were generally mottoes or emblematical devices. So the word here may be taken as including, more generally, any sententious sayings ; one of which Job at once proceeds to quote.

[4] Heb., אֵיד (*eyd*) *calamity* as in *v.* 17.

[5] Heb., חָסַךְ (*chasak*) *to keep back, restrain.*   See note on ch. xvi. 6 and compare ch. xxxiii. 18.   The scope of this member shows the sense in which these two lines are to be taken.   The A.V. and R.V. both do violence to Job's whole argument, and make him say the very opposite of what he was contending for.

[6] Heb., *Graves ; i.e., the burying place.*

[7] Heb., יָבַל (*yaval*) *to lead along* (in a good sense); *to lead forth,* gently or with escort.   Here, the *Hophal* is used (as in *v.* 32) of being escorted with honour, etc.   Compare Isa. lv. 12. Ps. xlv. 14, 15.   Hence, in *v.* 30, *to lead forth* so as to escape.

[8] So R.V.

[9] Heb., *sweet ;* but the meaning may be extended to anything *gentle, light,* or *pleasant.*

[10] We have this idea of drawing out or lengthened train from Judges iv. 6-7, and Ps. xxviii. 3.

[11] Heb., *Vanity* or *worthlessness.*

ELIPHAZ.   THIRD AND LAST ADDRESS.

k⁷. (page 63) chap. xxii.

k7 | T¹ | 1-4. Argument (General). Concerning God.
            U | 5-9. Accusation (Particular).
               V | 10, 11. Punishment (Particular).

     T² | 12. Argument (General). Concerning God.
            U | 13, 14. Accusation (Particular).
              V | 15-20. Punishment (General).

     T³ | 21-30. Argument (Particular). Concerning God, and Job.

T¹. (above) chap. xxii. 1-4. *The argument. (General).*
Concerning God.

xxii. 1. Then answered ELIPHAZ, the Temanite, and said :
  2. Can man [1] be profitable [2] unto GOD ? [3]
    As a wise man can serve one like himself.
  3. To Shaddai is it gain, if thou art just ?
    Or any profit, if thy ways be pure ?
  4. From awe of thee [4] will He debate with thee ?
    Or, into judgment with thee will He go ?

U. (above) chap. xxii. 5-9. *Accusation of Job.*

  5. It may be that thy wickedness is great ?
    And without number thine iniquities ;
  6. That thou didst take thy brother's pledge for naught ;
    Or didst strip off the garments of the poor ; [5]

---

[1] Heb., גֶּבֶר (*gever*). See note on ch. iv. 17.

[2] Heb., סָכַן (*sakan*) *to dwell beside another, to become one's neighbour.* Hence, *to assist* and *be of service to another.* Comp. ch. xv. 3 ; xxxv. 3.

[3] Heb., *El.*

[4] Heb., *from thy fear : i.e., from fear of thee.*

[5] *i.e., the poorly clad.* Heb., *naked ; i.e., so as to leave them naked.* The figure is *Synecdoche* (of the whole) by which the whole is put for a part ; and *naked* is put for scantily clad.

7. Or, that thou didst not give the weary drink ;
   Or, from the hungry thou withheldest bread ;
8. [Thou may'st have said]
   　　　　　　　　　' The land is for the strong ' ;
   　' And, favoured men [alone] should dwell therein.'
9. Widows [thou may'st] have sent away unhelped,
   And robbed [1] the fatherless of their support.[2]

V. (page 127) xxii. 10, 11.　*Job's punishment.*

10. This may be why the snares are round thee spread,
    And terror cometh suddenly on thee,
11. [And why] the darkness [3] thou canst not explain,[4]
    [And why] the waterfloods [5] o'erwhelm thy soul.[6]

T [2]. (page 127) chap. xxii. 12.　*The argument. (General).*
Concerning God.

12. [Is not] Eloah high in Heav'n sublime ? [7]
    Behold the highest of the stars,[8] How high !

U. (page 127) chap. xxii. 13, 14.　*The accusation of Job.*

13. [And yet, may be] thou say'st
    　　　　　　　　' How doth GOD [9] know ?
    　' And through the thickest darkness, can He judge ?

---

[1] Heb., *broken* or *crushed.*

[2] Heb., *arm,* which is put by *Metonymy* (of the Cause), for the support procured by it. See the same phrase in Ps. xxxvii. 17. Ezek. xxx. 22, and compare ch. xi. 9. Ps. lxxvii. 15 ; lxxxiii. 8.

[3] *Darkness* is put by *Metonymy* (of Adjunct) for the trouble associated with it.

[4] Heb., *see,* in the sense of *perceive, understand,* or *explain.*

[5] Heb., *waterfloods,* put by *Metonymy* (of Adjunct) for calamities, or that which overwhelms.

[6] *Thy soul,* put by *Synecdoche* (of the Part) for *thyself.*

[7] Heb., גָּבֹהַּ (*gāvoah*) *height,* the emotional word. Hence, used of wonder, and well expressed by *sublime.*

[8] Heb., *the head of the stars.*

[9] Heb., *El.*

14.   ' Thick clouds enrobe Him, that He cannot see,
       ' Alone He walketh in the vault of heaven.'

V. (page 127) chap. xxii. 15-20. *Punishment (general).*

15. Oh that thou would'st consider well the way
    Which wicked men [1] of old have ever trod.
16. They who were snatched away [2] before their time,
    Their strong foundation swept,[3] as with a flood.
17. Who unto GOD [4] did say 'Depart from us ! '
    [And ask'd] What Shaddai could do to them!
18. Yet He it was who filled their homes with good.

    This way of wicked men is far from me.[5]
19. The righteous see that THEY may well rejoice ;
    The innocent will laugh at them [and say]
20.   ' Surely OUR substance hath not been destroyed ;
       ' While THEIR abundance is consumed with fire.'

T[3]. (page 127) chap. xxii. 21-30. *Argument. (Particular).*
           Concerning God, and Job.

21. Oh, now, make friends with Him,[6] and be at peace,
    For thereby blessing [7] shall upon thee come.
22. Receive, I pray, instruction from His mouth,
    And lay up [all] His words within thy heart.

---

1 Heb., *men of wickedness.*
2 Heb., *withered up.*
3 Heb., יָצַק *(yātzach) to pour out, fuse,* as metal *melted.* The reference being perhaps to Sodom and Gomorrah, rather than to the Flood.
4 Heb., *El.*
5 *i.e.,* I cannot account for it. Eliphaz here takes up the words of Job in ch. xxi. 16, and turns them against him. See note.

6 The *Hiphil* here, refers us back to verse 1, and Eliphaz now bases his appeal on what he there stated.
7 Some Codices with Aramaic, Septuagint, Syriac, and Vulgate read " Thy gain (or profit) shall be blessing." See Ginsburg's Text and note

23. To Shaddai return : submit thyself ; [1]
    [And], from thy tent [2] put far away thy sin,
24. Then thou shalt lay up treasure [3] as the dust,
    And [gold] of Ophir [4] as the pebble-stones.[5]
25. Yea, Shaddai shall be thy precious ores,
    And [His] great strength as silver [6] unto thee.
26. For then, in Shaddai thou'lt take delight,
    And to Eloah thou shalt lift thy face.
27. Then shalt thou pray to Him, and He will hear,
    And unto Him thou wilt perform thy vows.
28. The thing thou purposest shall come to pass :
    And over all thy ways the light shall shine.
29. When others are depressed, then thou shalt say
    ' Look up ! For, humble men [7] HE will exalt;
30. ' Yea, HE doth [ever] save the innocent.' [8]

——————— 9

Ev'n so shalt THOU [10] escape through cleanness of thy hands.

---

[1] So it should be with Septuagint. See Ginsburg's Text and note.

[2] So (singular) in many MSS., with four early printed editions, the Sept., Syr., and Vulg. Versions. But *plural* ("tents") in some Codices, with seven early printed editions. See Ginsburg's Text and note.

[3] Heb., בֶּצֶר *(betzer)* only in these two verses. The word denotes ore (gold or silver) in its unwrought state.

[4] Heb., *Ophir*, put by *Metonymy* for the gold that came from thence.

[5] Heb., *pebbles of the brook.*

[6] Heb., *silver of toilings.*

[7] Heb., *low,* or *owly of eyes; i.e., of humble looks.*

[8] So it should be, with Sept. See Ginsburg's Text and note.

[9] A slight pause.

[10] So it should be, with Aramaic, Sept., Syr., and Vulg. versions. See Ginsburg's Text and note.

JOB'S THIRD REPLY TO ELIPHAZ.

1⁸. (page 63) chaps. xxiii., xxiv.

1⁸ | w | xxiii. 1-10. God's Inscrutability.
    x | 11, 12. Job's Integrity.
  w | 13—xxiv. 1. God's Inscrutability.
    x | 2-25. Man's Iniquity.

---

w. (above) chap. xxiii. 1-10. *God's Inscrutability.*

w | l | 1-5. Job's wish for Trial.
  m | 6, 7. His confidence of the issue.
 l | 8, 9. Job's search for Trial.
  m | 10. His confidence of the issue.

---

x. (above) chap. xxiv. 2-25. *Man's Iniquity.*

x | o | 2-17. Crimes.
  p | 18-20. What the issue ought to be.
 o | 21, 22. Crimes.
  p | 23-25. What the issue commonly is.

---

l. (above) chap. xxiii. 1-5. *Job's wish for Trial.*

xxiii. 1. Then JOB answered [Eliphaz], and said :
    2. To-day again my plaint is bitter, still :
       His hand¹ is heavier far than all my groans.
    3. Oh, that I knew where I might find Him : knew
       How I might come unto His [judgment] seat !

---

¹ So it should be, with Sept., and Syr. See Ginsburg's Text and note. *Hand* is put by *Metonymy* for the calamity inflicted by it. Compare ch. xiii. 21 ; and xix. 21.

   4. I would set out my cause before His face ;
      And I would fill my mouth with arguments,
   5. And well I know how He would answer me,
      And understand what He, to me, would say.

     m. (page 131) chap. xxiii. 6, 7. *Job's Integrity.*

   6. Would He, with His great pow'r, contend with me ?
      Nay, but He would surely set on me His heart.
   7. There, I, an upright man, would plead with Him,
      And I, for ever from my Judge go free.

    l. (page 131) chap. xxiii. 8, 9. *Job's search for Trial.*

   8. Lo, to the East I go : He is not there ;
      And to the West, but I perceive Him not :
   9. Or North, where He doth work, I look in vain ;
      Or in the South, He hides where none can see.

m. (page 131) chap. xxiii. 10. *Job's confidence of the Issue.*

  10. But mine own chosen way He knoweth well ;
      If tried,[1] I know I should come forth as gold.

    x. (page 131) chap. xxiii. 11, 12. *Job's Integrity.*

  11. My foot hath held, fast firmly, to His steps ;
      His way I have observed ; nor gone aside.
  12. From His commands [2] I have not turnèd back ;
      Yea, in my heart,[3] I treasured up His words.[4]

w. (page 131) chaps. xxiii. 13—xxiv. 1. *God's Inscrutability.*

  13. But He is [God] alone :[5] Who turneth Him ?
      What He [6] desireth, even that He does.

---

[1] Heb., *if He would try me.*
[2] Heb., *the commandments of His lips.*
[3] Or, *in my bosom*, with Sept., and

Vulg. See Ginsburg's Text and note.
[4] Heb., *the words of His lips.*
[5] Heb., *He is one.*
[6] Heb., *His soul.*

14. What is decreed for me, He will perform :
And many such [decrees] He hath in store.[1]

15. [Shut out then] from His presence, I'm in fear ;
I think of Him and I am sore afraid.[2]

16. For, God [3] [it is] Who maketh faint my heart;
Yea, Shaddai it is Who troubleth me.

17. Not from the darkness [4] am I thus dismayed,
Nor yet because thick darkness [4] veils my face.[5]

xxiv. 1. Since, then, events [6] from Shaddai are not hid,
Why do not they who love [7] Him know [8] His ways ? [9]

x. (page 131) chap. xxiv. 2-25. *Man's Iniquity.*

o. (page 131) chap. xxiv. 2-17. *His crimes.*

2. [Ungodly men, their neighbours'] landmarks move ; [10]
They seize on flocks, and feed them [as their own].

3. [Some], from the fatherless, drive off their ass,
And take the widow's ox from her in pledge.

4. [While others] turn the needy from their way ;
And all the poor [and wretched] hide themselves.

5. Behold them! As wild-asses, they go forth,
And, on the plains, they early seek their prey ;
The barren steppe doth yield their children food.

---

1 Heb., *are with Him;* *i.e.*, laid up with him (for me).

2 Heb., פַּחַד *(pachad)* is a *Homonym.* Here, and Deut xxviii. 66, it means *to fear*, while in Is. ix. 5, Hos. iii. 5, it means (and should be rendered) *rejoice.*

3 Heb., *El.*

4 *Darkness* is put by *Metonymy* for *trouble* and *calamity.*

5 So R.V margin. The R.V. and A.V. text makes no intelligible sense, because it is entirely out of harmony with the scope of the whole member.

6 Heb., *times;* put by *Metonymy* (of adjunct) for *events* that take place

in them. Ps. xxxi. 15 ; 1 Ch. xii. 32 ; xxix. 30 ; Est. i. 13 ; 2 Tim. iii. 1.

7 Heb., *His knowers: i.e.*, those who are His and therefore love Him. See Ps. v. 12 ; ix. 11.

8 Heb., *see* in the sense of *perceive* or *understand.*

9 Heb., *days;* put by *Metonymy* (of the adjunct) for what is done in them : *e.g.*, His time of judgment or of visitation. See ch. xviii. 20. Ps. xxxvii 13 ; cxxxvii. 7. Ezek. xxi. 29. Obad. 12. Lu. xix. 42. 1 Cor. iv. 3.

10 See Deut. xix. 14 ; xxvii. 17 ; Prov. xxii. 28 ; xxiii. 10.

6. They reap [down corn] in fields which are not theirs; [1]
   The vineyard of the wicked they despoil.
7. Ill-clad, they [2] lodge [3] without a covering,
   And without any shelter from the cold.
8. With sweeping-rain from mountain-storm they're wet;
   For want of refuge they embrace a rock.
9. These [bad men] tear the orphan from the breast;
   That which is on the poor they take to pledge.
10. Stripped of their [scanty] clothing they [4] go forth,
    And, hungry, carry [their [5] task-masters'] sheaves.
11. Within their [5] walls, these poor, press out their [5] oil;
    Their [5] wine-presses they [4] tread, though suffering thirst.
12. From city, and from houses,[6] groans ascend;
    With shrieks, those being murdered [7] cry for help;
    Yet Ꮐ⊙Ᏸ [8] regards not this enormity!

———— [9]

13. [Others again] [10] revolt against the light; [11]
    They have no knowledge of its [blessèd] ways,
    Neither abide they in the paths thereof.
14. The murderer, at day-break, riseth up,
    That he may slay the poor and destitute;
    [And then again] at night he plays the thief.

———

1 Heb., בְּלִילֹו *(belēlō) his corn.* But if divided into two words it reads בְּלִי לֹו *(belē lō) not his own.* In this latter case there is the *Ellipsis* of the *accusative* case, which leaves what they reaped undefined. The R.V. defines it as *provender.*

2 We take it as plural, as the singular means *every one of them*: *i.e.,* all these lawless men.

3 Heb., *to pass the night.*

4 *They*: *i.e.,* the poor who are thus oppressed.

5 *Their*: *i.e.,* the wicked who oppress these poor.

6 So it should be with Sept. See Ginsburg's Text and note.

7 Heb., *the soul of the slain.*

8 Heb., *Eloah.*

9 A slight pause.

10 Heb., *they.*

11 *i.e.,* they hate it because of their evil deeds; and commit their sins in the darkness. A different class from those described above, who oppress openly by day; "children of the night."

15. Th' adulterer [1] for [midnight's] darkness [2] waits,
    No eye, he saith, shall see the path I take;
    And so he puts a covering on his face.
16. [Burglars] break into houses in the dark,
    Which they had set a mark on [3] in the day;
    For, they, the daylight do not love. [4]
17. For all such, light is as the shade of death ;
    For [in the light] death's [5] terrors they discern.

p. (page 131) chap. xxiv. 18-20.   *What the issue ought to be.*

18. Swift as the [rushing] waters' face, [so will]
    His cursèd portion vanish from the earth :
19. And he, to his own vineyard ne'er return.
    [Ev'n so] with those who sin will Sheol deal.
20. The womb which bore him doth forget him there ;
    The worm [doth love him and] doth find him sweet.
    He will not be remembered any more :
    The wicked man lies, shivered, like a tree.

o. (page 131) chap. xxiv. 21, 22.   *His crimes.*

21. [Again, the wicked] wrongs [6] the barren [wife] ; [7]
    And to the widow no compassion shows.
22. And also by his might he drags the strong away :
    He riseth up, no one is sure of life.

---

[1] Heb., *the eye of the adulterer.*

[2] Heb., נֶשֶׁף (*nesheph*) is a *Homonym*, and means (1) darkness, (2) daylight. Here (and Prov. vii. 9. 2 Kings vii. 5, 7. Isa. v. 11 ; xxi. 4 ; lix. 10, and Jer. xiii. 6, 16, it is *darkness*). But in Job vii. 4. 1 Sam. xxx. 17. Ps. cxix. 147, it is *daylight*).

[3] Heb., *have sealed for themselves;* either sealed the house in their minds; or, as R.V., sealed or *shut themselves up in the daytime.*

[4] Heb., *know.* See John iii. 19-21. Jer. xlix. 9. Obad. 5. Matt. xxvii. 64.

[5] *i.e.,* the terrors of the shadow of death : the Heb. word being repeated in the second line.

[6] Or *plunders.*

[7] The barren wife was considered more helpless than the widow, as the latter might have sons to help her.

p. (page 131) chap. **xxiv**. 23-25).   *What the issue commonly is.*

23. [God] lets them rest secure, and confident :
Though still His eyes are ever on their ways.
24. They tower a little while, and then are gone ;
Brought low, they're gathered in as others are ;
Or cut off, even as the ears of corn.
25. If this be not so, who can prove me wrong ?
Or make my words to be of no account ?

BILDAD'S THIRD (AND LAST) ADDRESS.

k⁸. (page 63) chap. xxv.

k⁸ | Y | 1-3. God. His omnipotence.
    | Z | 4-6. Man. His impotence.

Y. (above) chap. xxv. 1-3. *God. His omnipotence.*

1. Then answered BILDAD, the Shuite, and said :
   With HIM, Dominion is, and reverence ;
2. 'Tis He who maketh harmony [1] on high.
3. And, of His hosts, the number, who can count ?
   Yea, upon whom ariseth not His light ? [2]

Z. (above) chap. xxv. 4-6. *Man. His impotence.*

4. How then can mortal man [3] be just with GOD ? [4]
   Or, he be pure, who is of woman born ?
5. Behold the moon : to Him [5] it shineth not ;
   [Yea], e'en the stars, in His sight, are not pure.
6. How much less mortal man—[the food of] worms—
   Or any son of man—himself a worm !

---

[1] Heb., שָׁלוֹם *(shalōm)*, *peace*. As this refers to all in the heavens— *things* as well as *beings*—" harmony " seems better to agree with the beauty and order of all in the heavens.

[2] The first line relates to things in heaven ; the second to things on Earth.

[3] See note on ch. iv. 17.

[4] Heb., *El.*

[5] Some codices, with six early printed Editions, and Aramaic and Syriac Versions, omit the " and." See Ginsburg's Heb. Text and note.

JOB'S REPLY TO BILDAD'S THIRD (AND LAST) ADDRESS.

1⁸. (page 63) chaps. xxvi. 1—xxvii. 10.

1⁸ | A | xxvi. 1-4.   Appeal to his Friends.
  B | 5-14.   God's ways : His Power incomparable.
  A | xxvii. 1-4.   Appeal to his Friends.
    B | 5-10.   Job's ways : his Righteousness incomparable.

A. (above) chap. xxvi. 1-4.   *Appeal to his Friends.*

1. But Job answered [Bildad] and said,
2. How hast thou helpèd him who hath no pow'r?
   Or succour brought to him who hath no strength?[1]
3. How hast thou counselled him who is unlearned?
   Or wisdom hast abundantly made known?[2]
4. By[3] whom hast thou [been taught][4] to speak these words?
   Whose inspiration hath come forth to thee?[5]

B. (above) chap. xxvi. 5-14.   *God's ways. His power incomparable.*

5. [Where] rest[6] the [mighty] Rephaim[7] of old?—

---

[1] Heb., *arm,* put by *Metonymy* for *strength,* or *power.*

[2] Referring ironically to Bildad's very brief address.

[3] Heb., אֶת־מִי (*eth-mī*) *with whom; i.e., by the aid of whom.*

[4] The *Ellipsis* may well be thus supplied from the next line.

[5] Referring perhaps to Bildad's few words which are a poor repetition of what Eliphaz had better said already: as if inspired by him Job at once proceeds to surpass Bildad's description of God's power.

[6] Heb., חוּל (*chūl*) may thus rendered, as in Hos. xi. 6 (*abide*). Gen. viii. 10 (*stayed*). Judg. iii. 25 (*tarried*). 2 Sam. iii. 29 (*rest*). Job xxxv. 14 (*wait*).

[7] The *Rephaim* were probably akin to the *Nephilim* of Gen. vi. 4.

These *Nephilim* were the awful progeny of the fallen angels with women. (See Gen. vi. 1, 2, Jude 6-8, and 2 Pet. ii. 4, 5): hence called (*Nephilim*) *fallen ones,* from נָפַל (*naphal*) *to fall* (not "giants"). These had all to be destroyed by the Flood. But there was a second irruption "also after that" (Gen. vi. 4) and the progeny seems to have been called *Rephaim* (translated "giants"). These settled in Canaan (Gen. xv. 20) and had to be destroyed. Hence Israel had to exterminate them. Moses destroyed some (Num. xiii. 28) and David destroyed the last of them (1 Ch. xx). They appear to have no resurrection (Is. xxvi. 14 "they are *Rephaim*, they shall not rise. But the Earth shall "cast them out" (*v.* 19).)

Beneath the sea and things that are therein !—

6. [Open] before Him, naked Sheol lies,
   And deep Abaddon,[1] hath no covering.

7. The North He stretches o'er the empty space,[2]
   And hangeth not the Earth on anything.[3]

8. He bindeth up the waters in thick clouds,
   And [yet] the cloud is not rent under them.[4]

9. He closeth fast [5] the entrance [6] to His throne,
   And over it He spreadeth His dark cloud.

10. The round horizon [7] bounds the waters' face,
    And there the fading light with darkness blends.

11. Heaven's pillars [mountains great], He makes to rock ; [8]
    And they are terrified at His rebuke.[9]

12. By His great pow'r He calms the [raging] sea ;
    And by His wisdom He subdues its pride.

13. The heav'ns so fair His spirit [10] beautified,
    The Serpent [constellation] He revolves.

14. Lo, these are only outlines of His way,[11]
    'Tis but a whisper [12] that we hear of Him,
    His wondrous pow'r,[13] then, who can comprehend ?

---

[1] *Abaddon* means *destruction*, and is another name for *Sheol* because it is the place of destruction. Compare chap. xxxi. 12, and Prov. xxvii. 20.

[2] Heb., *Tohu*, desolation ; As in Gen. i. 2. " Without form."

[3] Heb., בְּלִי־מָה (*belīmah*) *not what :* i.e., *not anything*.

[4] Some codices quoted in the Massorah with Aramaic and Septuagint, and one early printed Edition read " it " or " him." See Ginsburg's Text and note. The " it " in this case would refer to the weight.

[5] Compare Ps. xcvii. 2.

[6] Or *presence.* Heb., *face.*

[7] Heb., *He hath rounded off,* or *encircled.*

[8] Or, *oscillate.* Heb., *are shaken,* or *rocked.*

[9] *i.e.*, at the voice of His thunder.

[10] Compare Ps. xxxiii. 6.

[11] So it is to be *read.* It is *written* " ways " (pl.). In some codices, with Septuagint, it is *sing*, both written and read. In others, with five early printed Editions, Aramaic, Syriac, and Vulgate, it is both *written* and *read* " ways " (pl.). See Ginsburg's Text and notes.

[12] Compare i. Kings xix. 12.

[13] Heb., *the thunder of His power,* i.e., *mighty power.*

A. (page 138) chap. **xxvii.** 1-4. *Appeal to his Friends.*

1. Moreover Job continued his address, and said :
2. As God[1] doth live[2] Who takes away my right,
    Ev'n Shaddai, who hath embittered me,[3]
3. So long as breath remaineth in [my mouth],[4]
    And in my nostrils is Eloah's breath,[5]
4. These lips of mine shall not perverseness speak,—
    My tongue shall never utter what is false.

B. (page 138) chap. xxvii. 5-10. *Job's ways : his righteousness incomparable.*

5. No, no ;[6] I'll not admit you to be right,
    Nor, while I live,[7] my innocence let go ;[8]
6. My right[9] I hold ; I will not give it up !
    My heart shall not reproach me all my days.[10]
7. Ev'n were the Evil One mine enemy,
    And, he—th' Unjust should my accuser be.
8. For, what hope hath the godless man, or gain ?
    When once Eloah doth demand his life[11]
9. Will God[12] [indeed] give ear unto his cry
    When [trouble or] distress shall come on him ?
10. [No], he's not one who joys in Shaddai !
    Or calls, at any time, on Eloah !

---

[1] Heb., *El.*
[2] A well-known Heb. **form** of adjuration. Only used here (once) by Job.
[3] Heb., *my soul.*
[4] Heb., *to me.*
[5] Compare Gen. ii. 7, **and ch.** xxxiii. 4.
[6] Heb., *far be it from me.*

[7] Heb., *till my last gasp.*
[8] *i.e.,* let it be taken from me.
[9] Or *righteousness.*
[10] Heb., *any one of my days.*
[11] Heb., *nephesh.* Compare Matt. xvi. 26, and see note **in Ginsburg's** Heb. Text.
[12] Heb. *El.*

ZOPHAR'S THIRD (AND LAST) ADDRESS.*

k⁹. (page 63) chaps. xxvii. 11—xxviii. 28.

k⁹   C | xxvii. 11-23.   Unwisdom.

    D | a | xxviii. 1-6.   What man knows.

        b | 7, 8.   What man does NOT know.

    D | a | 9-11.   What man can do.

        b | 12-19.   What man can NOT do.

  C | 20-28.   Wisdom.

---

*In assigning a third discourse to Zophar we are not alone: for Dr. Kennicott (*Remarks on select passages of the Old Testament,* Oxford, 1787, pp. 169, 170), apportions chap. xxvii. 13—xxviii. 28; and Prof. Hermann Bernard, of Cambridge, *Comm.* in loco; and Wolfshon (whom he quotes) assign chap. xxvii. 13—xxviii. 28. We differ with these commentators only by commencing at verse 11 instead of verse 13; and our readers must judge for themselves.

That a third address must be assigned to Zophar seems clear from the following considerations :—

1. The symmetry of the structure of this portion of the book demands it. (See page 63.)

2. The sentiments expressed (xxvii. 11—xxviii. 28) demand it, for they are the very opposite of what Job asserted and maintained to the very end. The perplexity of the commentators is proof of this.

3. Moreover, these sentiments agree exactly with what Zophar had been maintaining all through.

Indeed, he commences his third address (xxvii. 13) with the very words which concluded his second address (chap. xx. 29). It is incredible that Job could thus adopt the very argument he was opposing, without a word to indicate that his views had thus suddenly changed.

4. If these are the words of Job, then his friends had evidently "convinced" him; which was the very thing Elihu declared *they had not done* (see chap. xxxii. 12).

5. The Hebrew of xxix. 1 does not require it. It reads, "Job added to take up his discourse, and said" (see A.V. margin). This may mean *conclusion* just as well as continuation. Indeed it marks off chaps. xxix.—xxxi. as not being one of the series of replies, but as the formal conclusion of the whole (Z) corresponding with chap. iii. (Z) which was the formal opening of the whole. We are thus prepared for the sentence with which the member Z is closed, "The words of Job are ended" (xxxi. 40).

C. (page 141) chap. xxvii. 11-23. *Unwisdom.*

xxvii. 11. I would now speak about the ways [1] of GOD ; [2]
   And Shaddai's dealings [3] [with you] not conceal.
   12. Ye, surely, must have seen them for yourselves ;
      Or, are ye then, so altogether vain ? [4]
   13. THIS is the lot of wicked men from GOD [5]
      Th' oppressor's heritage from Shaddai's hand : [6]
   14. If children multiply : 'tis for the sword :
      Of bread, his offspring will not have enough.
   15. Their issue [7] will be buried at their death, [8]
      But, widows will not lamentation make.
   16. Though silver, like the dust, he should heap up,
      And garments make in number like the sand ;
   17. Though he prepare ! the just will put it on ;
      His silver will the innocent divide.
   18. The house he builds : 'tis frail as is the moth's ; [9]
      Or, as the booth which vineyard watcher makes. [10]

---

[1] Heb., *by the hand of God :* " hand "
being put by *Metonymy* for what
is done by His hand or power.
Zophar is speaking of God's *mode* of
working ; *i.e.,* His *ways*, rendered
dealings in the next line (compare
R.V.).

[2] Heb., *El*, taking up the two
titles used by Job in verses 9 and 10.

[3] Heb., *that which is with the
Almighty.* The preposition עִם (*îm*)
with, is often used to denote some
special *attribute*, or *way.* See chap.
xii. 16, *with Him* is strength and
wisdom. So chap. xv. 9 ; xxiii. 14.

[4] Heb., *vain with vanity, i.e.,* ye must
have observed God's ways ; or, have
ye seen them all to no purpose ?
Hence Zophar here first shows

God's ways in dealing with the
wicked who manifest their unwisdom in not fearing Him or
departing from evil.

[5] Heb., *El.*

[6] Referring to *the hand of God* in
v. 11.

[7] Heb., *those that remain of him,
his survivors.*

[8] מָוֶת with the art., as here means
judicial death.

[9] *i.e.,* not as the moth builds, but
like it in its frailty, as the watcher's
booth in the following line which
gives a corresponding sense.

[10] Compare Is. i. 8. Jonah iv. 5 ;
Lev. xxiii. 40-42. Generally made
of branches of trees.

19. He lies down rich, [his wealth] not gathered in : [1]
    He openeth his eyes, and it is gone! [2]
20. Terrors will overtake him as a flood;
    A whirlwind in the night will sweep him off.
21. The east wind catcheth him, and he is gone;
    Yea, as a storm it hurls him from his place.
22. He,[3] who before, was wont to flee from him,[4]
    Will now come down [5] on him, and will not spare,
23. In triumph he will clap his hands at him;
    And hiss him forth from out his dwelling-place.[6]

———— [7]

---

[1] Heb. Text וְלֹא יֵאָסֵף (*velō yeah-seyph*) *it is not gathered in; i.e.*, his wealth, which is all put out in trade, or at interest, and not all collected or gathered in. According to another reading וְלֹא יֹסִיף (*velō yosīf*) *it is not added to.* The Syriac and Septuagint agree with this reading. (lxx= καὶ οὐ προσθήσει *kai ou prosthesei*). See Ginsburg's Text and note.

To take these two lines as referring to the man instead of to his wealth, is to quite miss the point, and make the expression yield no sense. The word "rich" naturally suggests the supply of the *Ellipsis* by "his wealth."

[2] Heb., *it is not; i.e.*, his wealth. To render it "he is not" (A.V. and R.V.) is contrary to the sense. For if he lives to wake up the man *is*. But if "he is not," then he dies, instead of opening his eyes.

[3] To supply the word "*God*," here, in italics as is done by the A.V. and R.V., introduces confusion. There is no need to add anything to the Hebrew. "He," *i.e.*, the man who used to flee in fear from the wicked man in his prosperity, now casts himself against him and takes his revenge when his oppressor has been brought low.

[4] Heb., *used hastily to flee from his hand* ("hand" being put by *Metonymy* for *power*.

[5] Heb., *casteth himself upon him.* But there are many ways in which this can be done, without making a physical assault; and all are included in this English idiom. We have rendered it, therefore, as above. Our phrase is eminently idiomatic, and eloquently expresses the sense of the Hebrew.

[6] Could Job, who held such sentiments as those expressed in chaps. xii. 6, and xxi. 7-12, have ever uttered these words of chap. xxvii. 13-23 ? They are exactly the opposite, and are the arguments of all his three friends. If this is Job's address, then he had quite changed his views, and *had been convinced* by his friends; which is the very thing they they are charged with not having done. Elihu in chap. xxxii. 12 distinctly says :

"But lo, not one of you convincèd Job;

Not one, who really answered what he said."

This seems to complete the evidence for considering chaps. xxvii. 11—xxviii. 28, the third, and last, discourse of Zophar.

[7] A slight pause to be made here.

a. (page 141) chap. xxviii. 1-6.   *What man knows.*

1. Yes [1]—truly—for the silver there's a vein ;
   A place also for gold which they refine.

2. Iron may be brought up from out the earth ; [2]
   And copper may be smelted from the ore.

3. To darkness ['neath the earth] man sets a bound ; [3]
   In all directions [4] he explores [beneath],
   Yea, ev'n the ores of earth [5] in darkness [hid].

4. A shaft he sinks,[6] 'neath where the settler dwells,[7]
   And there, forgotten by the well-worn way,[8]
   Let themselves down and pass away [from men].

5. As for the earth, bread cometh forth from it :
   Yet underneath it fire is stirrèd up.

6. Among its stones are glowing sapphires found;
   And in its dust are nuggets of pure gold.

b. (page 141) chap. xxviii. 7, 8.   *What man does not know.*

7. There is a path no bird of prey hath known ;
   Nor hath the eagle's eye discovered it.

8. [A path] which no proud beast [9] hath ever trod;
   Not [10] e'en the lion ever passed that way.

---

1 This rendering covers the abrupt change of thought, as to what man, though so unwise as to his own best interest, yet knows and can do in connection with his material and temporal interests. The change is marked by the causal כִּי (*kî*) *for,*= *for truly.*

2 Heb., עָפָר (aphar) the *interior* or *deep* ground. Not the surface as in xxxix. 14 ; xli. 33.

3 By sinking a shaft and introducing light.

4 Heb., *to every extremity*, or *to each point : i.e., in all directions.* Compare Ezek. v. 10.

5 Heb., *stones of darkness : i e.,* stones hidden in the darkness beneath the earth.

6 Heb., נַחַל (*nachal*) a *wady* or *torrent bed.* The context shows that it must be *a shaft* that is meant.

7 Heb., גֵּר (*gahr*) *stranger pilgrim,* one away from home (Lev. xvii. 12). Exactly what is expressed by our modern word " settler."

8 Heb., *forgotten of the foot : foot* being put by *Metonymy* for *foot-path.* The way itself is personified as forgetting them, as in chap. vii. 10. Ps. ciii. 16.

9 Heb., *sons of pride : i.e.,* ravenous beasts.

10 Or, " *and not.*" See Ginsburg's Text, and note.

a. (page 141) ch. xxviii. 9-11. *What man can do.*

9. Man lays his hand upon the flinty rock ;
   The hills he overturneth by their roots.
10. He cutteth water-channels in the rocks ;
   His eye detecteth every precious thing.
11. The over-flowing floods he doth restrain ;
   The hidden things he bringeth forth to light.

b. (page 141) chap. xxviii. 12-19. *What man can not do.*

12. But wisdom—whence can it be [thus] obtained ?
   And understanding : where the place thereof ?
13. No mortal man doth know the way [1] thereto ;
   Among the living [2] it can not found.
14. Th' abyss exclaims ' [Wisdom] is not in me.'
   And ocean roars—' Nor with me dwelleth[3] it.'
15. Fine gold cannot be given in its stead,
   Neither can silver for its price be weighed.
16. With Ophir's gold it never can be bought ;
   Nor with the onyx or the sapphire gem.
17. Crystal and gold cannot compare with it ;
   Nor vessels [4] of pure gold be its exchange.
18. Corals and diamonds [5] can not be named ;
   The worth of wisdom far excelleth pearls.
19. The topaz gem of Cush equals it not ;
   And purest gold with it can not be weighed.

---

[1] So it should be, with Sept. See Ginsburg's Text, and note.

[2] Heb., *in the land of the living.*

[3] In the second line the negative is stronger than in the first : *i.e., it is nowhere with me*, it is well expressed by the word *dwelleth*.

Some codices, with one early printed Edition, Aramaic, Sept. and Vulgate Versions read it plural. See Ginsburg's Text and note.

[5] It is difficult, if not impossible to determine with certainty the particular gems meant, as they are proper names, and these are not the same in any two languages.

C. (page 141) chap. xxviii. 20-28. *Wisdom.*

20. Whence, then, this wisdom ? [Whence, then] doth it
   come ?
   And understanding ; Where the place thereof?
21. So hidden from the eyes of all who live ;
   And from the birds of heav'n so close concealed.
22. Death and Destruction [both alike] declare
   ' Only a rumour of it reach'd our ears.'
23. But Eloah hath understood the way ;
   And He discerns the [secret] place thereof.
24. For HE can look to Earth's remotest bounds,
   And all beneath the heavens He beholds.
25. So that He gives the air its gravity ;
   And waters meteth out by measurement.
26. When for the rain He gave forth a decree
   A way appointed for the thunder-flash.
27. Then did He see it, and declare it [good] ;
   Yea, He established [1] it and showed it forth [2]
28. But He unto the sons of Adam saith,
      ' Lo ! Wisdom is to reverence the Lord ; [3]
      ' And understanding is to flee from sin.' [4]

---

[1] Some codices (with five early printed editions) read " marked." See Ginsburg's Heb. Text and note.

[2] Or, *set it up before Himself : i.e.*, set it up for contemplation and searching out by man.

[3] Heb., *Adonai : i.e.*, the Lord, as ruling on earth. Many MSS. and old Editions read *Jehovah*, and the Massorah includes this among the 134 passages where *Adonai* is to be read, though it should be written Jehovah.

[4] This is not Divine *wisdom*. It is human *policy*. True wisdom ever justifies God and condemns one's self. This includes the other. We may fear the Lord without justifying Him, and we may depart from evil without condemning ourselves. But, on the other hand, we cannot justify God without reverencing Him ; and we cannot condemn ourselves without departing from the evil we deplore. See the notes on this pages, 24-26.

JOB'S JUSTIFICATION.   (CONCLUSION.)

Z. (page 63) chap. xxix—xxxi.

Z | E | **xxix.**   Saddened retrospect of past Prosperity.
   F | **xxx.**   Sorrowful description of present Misery.
   G | **xxxi.**   Solemn asseveration of Innocence.

E. (above) chap. xxix.   *Saddened retrospect of his past Prosperity.*

E | H | c | 1-6.   Job's prosperity.   (What he was.)
   d | 7-11.   His honour.

   I | e | 12.   Redress of wrong ⎫
      f | 13.   Beneficence ⎪
         g | 14-.   Righteousness ⎬ What
   I | *g* | -14.   Justice ⎪ Job
      f | 15, 16.   Beneficence ⎪ did.
   e | 17.   Redress of wrong ⎭

   H | c | 18-20.   Job's prosperity.   (What he thought.)
   d | 21-25.   His honour.

c. (page 147) chap. **xxix.** 1-6. *Job's prosperity. What he was.*

  1. Then JOB resumed[1] [and concluded] his [original]
     address (chap. iii).

  2. Oh that I were as in the olden times;[2]
     As in the days when **GOD**[3] watched over me.

  3. When shone His lamp so brightly o'er my head,
     And, by His light, I could in darkness walk.

  4. As did I in the spring-time[4] of my life,
     With **GOD'S**[3] own secret presence[5] in my tent.

  5. When Shaddai was yet with me, my stay,[6]
     And round me were my children in their youth.

  6. When with th' abundant[7] milk my feet I bathed,
     And oil from out the rock flowed forth for me.

d. (page 147) chap. **xxix.** 7-11. *Job's honour.*

  7. When to the city's gate I made my way,
     And in the open place prepared my seat,

  8. The young men saw me, and withdrew[8] themselves,
     Yea, all the elders would rise up and stand.

  9. The rulers too, from talking would refrain,
     And used to lay their hand upon their mouth.

---

[1] Heb,, וַיֹּסֶף (*vayyoseph*) *and he added:* added to *take up.* This certainly indicates more than a pause. It marks a change. What follows is no mere reply to Zophar's last address. Job takes up his original complaint in ch. iii., and answers all that his three Friends had said, by reviewing his whole past and present life. This last member *Z* (xxix.—xxxi.) corresponds with the first member of this division Z (iii.).

[2] Heb., *months of old.*

[3] Heb., *Eloah.*

[4] Heb., *autumn.* But as the ancient year began in our autumn, so the word has reference to the *beginning* of the year, and corresponds with our Spring. Hence we speak of " the spring-time of youth."

[5] Heb., סוֹד (*sūd*) *secret.* The secret of Jehovah implies all that is included in His *favour.* (See Ps. lv. 15. Job xix. 19. Here it denotes familiar intercourse.

[6] The Heb. עִמָּדִי (*immādi*) *with me,* implies intimate and constant communion. So Ps. xxiii. 4.

[7] The Figure of *milk* and *oil* denotes exuberance; and the word *abundant* well expresses it.

[8] Not " *hid themselves* " as A.V. and R.V. but *retired.*

10. The nobles' voice was hush'd ; they held their peace,
    Their tongue, in silence, to their palate [1] clave ;
11. The ear that heard of me pronounced me blessed ;
    The eye that saw, bore witness unto me,

I. (page 147) chap. xxix. 12-17. *Reasons. What Job did.*

(e. *Redress of wrong.*)

12. That I did save [2] the poor who crièd out,
    The fatherless, and him who had no help,

(f. *Beneficence.*)

13. The perishing to me his blessing gave ;
    I caused the widow's heart to sing for joy.

(g. *Righteousness.*)

14. My righteousness I put on as my clothes :

(g. *Justice.*)

My justice, as my robe and diadem,

(f. *Beneficence.*)

15. I was instead of eyes unto the blind,
    And to the lame I was instead of feet.
16. A father I was to the needy ones.
    The cause I did not know,[3] I searchèd out.

(e. *Redress of wrong.*)

17. I used to break the jaws [4] of evil men,
    And pluck the prey out of their very teeth.

---

[1] This is even more literal to the words than the A.V. and R.V.

[2] Heb., *used to deliver.*

[3] *i.e.*, the cause unknown: not the person, It is not merely impartiality that is meant, but carefulness to execute justice.

[4] Compare Ps. iii. 7 ; lviii. 6. Lam. iii. 16.

c. (page 147) ch. xxix. 18-20. *Job's prosperity.* (*What he thought*).

18. I said, I shall grow old as doth the palm; [1]
    Yea, multiplied like sand, my days shall be.
19. My root unto the waters shall spread out,[2]
    And all night long the dew be on my branch.
20. My glory, shall remain with me, still fresh :
    My bow, within my hand, renew its strength.[3]

d. (page 147) ch. xxix. 21-25. *Job's honour.*

21. To me, men hearkened, waited, and gave ear ;
    And at my counsel they did silence keep.
22. When I had spoken, none replied again ;
    So that on them my wisdom [4] still might fall.[5]
23. Yea, they would wait, as men for showers wait,
    And open wide their mouths, as for the rain.
24. That I should mock [6] them they would ne'er believe,
    Nor would they cause a shadow on my face,
25. I used to choose their way ; and sat as chief;
    As king among his subjects, so I dwelt ;
    And among mourners, as a comforter.

---

[1] The note in Ginsburg's Text, gives *branch.* Sept. has *palm-branch.*

[2] Heb., *opened out.*

[3] Heb., תַּחֲלִיף (*tachalĭph*) *regerminate.* See ch. xiv. 7, and compare ch. xxx. 11. See also Ps. cii. 27. Isa. ix. 9.

[4] Heb., *speech,* but *wise* utterances, are clearly meant, from the context of the words and scope of the passage.

[5] Compare Deut. xxxii. 2.

[6] As in ch. xii. 4.

F. (page 147) chap. **xxx.** *Sorrowful description of his present Misery.*

F | J | 1-14. From others. (1-8, their character. 9-14, their conduct.)

K | 15-18. In himself. (15, 16, mental. 17-19, bodily).

J | 19-24. From God. (20, silence. 21-24, action.)

K | 25-31. In himself.

J. (above) chap. **xxx.** 1-14. *From others : (Their character, vv.* 1-8 ; *their conduct, vv.* 9-14).

Their Character, vv. 1-8.

1. But, now, I'm held in scorn by younger men
   Whose fathers I would have disdained to put
   On level with the dogs that watch'd my flock.
2. What profit would their strength be unto me,
   When they had lost their ripened manhood's powers?
3. Through hunger[1] they were like the barren[2] rock.
   These vagrants[3] driven from the land of drought[4]
   For ages past[5] a desolation, wild,

---

[1] Heb., *want and hunger.*

[2] Compare Job iii. 7 ; xv. 34. Isa. xlix. 21. Lit., *they are a bare stiff rock.*

[3] עָרַק (*āhrak*) as a verb occurs only here. In Syriac it means *to flee.* In Arabic it means *to roam.* Hence of the gnawing of fugitive or darting pains (compare the noun or participle in verse 17). The word may well be rendered *vagrants*, roaming to and fro from the desert to the borders of civilization through want.

[4] Compare ch. xxiv. 19. Ps. lxx. 2 ; cvii. 35.

[5] Heb., *yesterday* or *yesternight.* See Gen. xix. 34 ; xxxi. 29. 1 Kings xii. 26. Used idiomatically for the ages past and gone. See Ps. xc. 14, and compare Heb. xiii. 8. The indefiniteness of *time* in this line corresponds with the indefiniteness of *place* in the previous line.

4. Who 'mong the bushes pluck th' ill-tasting [1] herb
   And make the roots of juniper [2] their food.
5. From human intercourse [3] they're driven forth ;
   [And] men cry after them, as after thieves.[4]
6. In dark ravines they make their dwelling place.
   In holes of earth,[5] and caverns of the rocks [6]
7. Among the desert scrub [7] they raise their shouts [8]
   [And] under bramble bushes herd [like beasts]
8. Children of fools, yea, sons without a name,
   As outcasts they are driven from the land.

Their Conduct (ch. xxx. 9-14).

9. BUT, NOW, I have become their mocking-song ;
   Yea, I've become a by-word unto them.
10. They [all] abhor, and stand aloof from me ;
    And spare not now to spit before my face.[9]
11. Since HE hath loosed my [10] bow,[11] and humbled me,
    THEY too, before me, cast off all restraint.[12]
12. At my right hand this rabble brood rise up,
    They thrust aside my feet : [leave me no room].
    Against me they oppose [13] their hostile [14] ways.
13. They mar my path : [my movements they impede [15]] ;
    They seek my hurt, although it helps them not.[16]

---

[1] Various meanings are given to these proper nouns, about which there is necessarily great uncertainty in all languages. The etymology of this word points to any acrid herb.

[2] A.V. *mallows* ; R.V., *salt-wort*.

[3] Heb., *from the body : i.e.,* from the *body of men,* or *society.*

[4] Heb., *as the thief.*

[5] Artificial holes.

[6] Natural caverns.

[7] Heb., *bushes.*

[8] Heb., *bray.*

[9] Compare Deut. xxv. 9, Matt. xxvi. 67 ; xxvii. 30, &c.

[10] Written " his " : to be read " my."

[11] Or, *bow-string.* Compare chap. xxix. 20, to which this refers, by way of contrast.

[12] Heb., *let loose their bridle.*

[13] Heb., *cast up* as an earthwork.

[14] Heb., *the ways of destruction : i.e.,* hostile. The figure denotes military operations.

[15] This sentence we have inserted by way of an explanatory repetition.

[16] Lit., *no helper to them.*

14. As [waters] through a breach, they come [on me] ;
   And on me like a tempest they rush in.

K. (page 151) ch. xxx. 15-19. *Job's miseries. In himself.*
   Mental sufferings (vv. 15, 16).

15. All now is overthrown : [1] and, like the wind,
   Terrors my dignity have scatterèd
   And gone, like clouds [2] is my prosperity.
16. And now, my soul, within me is poured out,
   The days of my affliction hold me fast.

Bodily sufferings (vv. 17, 18).

17. By night by bones are pierced [with pains] without ; [3]
   My throbbing nerves [4] [within [5] me] never rest.
18. By great exertion [6] is my garment changed ;
   It girds me like the collar of my coat.[7]

J. (page 151) ch. xxx. 19-24. *Job's miseries. From God.*

19. Into the mire His hand [8] hath cast me down ;
   To dust and ashes I may be compared.
20. I cry aloud to Thee ; Thou answ'rest not ;
   I stand [in prayer] ; but Thou dost not regard.
21. Thou art become relentless [to my prayer] ;
   And dost assail me with Thy mighty hand.
22. Thou usedst to lift me up upon the wind,
   [Yea] Thou didst cause me [thereupon] to ride ;
   [But now,] Thy storm doth carry me away.

---

[1] The Heb. denotes *a complete over-throw.*

[2] Heb., *a thick cloud.*

[3] Heb. מֵעָלָי (*meyahlahĭ*) *from off* or *from above, i.e., upon me.*

[4] See note on verse 3, above.

[5] This must be supplied in contrast with the word " without " in the previous line.

[6] Heb., *with greatness of strength.*

[7] Heb., *like the mouth of, i.e.,* the opening, or collar of my coat. My garment, otherwise loose, clings like a tight collar.

[8] Heb., *He.*

23. I know that Thou wilt bring[1] me back to death,—
    E'en to the place ordain'd for all who live.[2]
24. Ah! prayer [for these] is vain.[3]   He will not help,[4]
    Though when in trouble one may cry for them.

K. (page 151) ch. xxx. 25-31. *Job's misery. In himself.*

25. Did I not weep for him whose lot was hard?[5]
    Was I not sorely grievèd[6] for the poor?
26. Yet, when I looked for good, then evil came;
    And darkness [deep] when I expected light.
27. My bowels boil;[7] and they are never still;
    So suddenly has trouble[8] come on me.[9]
28. Even in gloom[10] I go, without the sun.
    I rose up in th' assembly, and cried "Help"!
29. A brother I became to howling brutes
    And a companion to the birds that screech.
30. Without: my skin is burnt up and is black;[11]
    Within: my bones are all consumed with heat.
31. Therefore my harp, to mourning, has been turned;
    My lyre, is like the voice of them that weep.

---

[1] Heb., שׁוּב (*shūv*) *to return*, referring to Gen. iii. 19, and to his own words in ch. i. 21. Compare ch. xxxiv. 15. Ecc. xii. 7. Ps. xc. 3.

[2] Compare Heb. ix. 27.

[3] Heb., לֹא־בְּעִי (*lo-behi*) *no prayer*. The negative thus united means *prayerless*, like our prefixes *un-*, *in-*, *im-*. Only we have no English use of such prefixes with the word prayer. "Prayer is of no avail" is the meaning of the words.

[4] Heb., *He will not put forth his hand.*

[5] Heb., *for the hard of day:* a day of calamity.

[6] Heb., עֲגַם (*āgam*) *to be troubled*. Only here.

[7] Heb., *caused to boil*. This is the force of the *Pual*.

[8] Heb., *days of affliction*.

[9] Heb., *prevented*, or *anticipated* me. This suggests the idea of *suddenness*.

[10] Darkness or blackness is put by *Metonymy* for mourning.

[11] Heb., *from upon me;* i.e., without, the outside being contrasted with the bones beneath the skin.

G. (page 147) chap. xxxi. *Solemn asseveration of his innocence,
in respect to various sins.*

G | L¹ | h¹ | 1. Sin. (Unchastity.)
| | | i¹ | 2-4. Consequence.
| | L² | h² | 5. Sin. (Deceit.)
| | | i² | 6. Consequence. (Trial desired.)
| | L³ | h³ | 7. Sin. (Dishonesty.)
| | | i³ | 8. Consequence. (Imprecation.)
| | L⁴ | h⁴ | 9. Sin. (Adultery.)
| | | i⁴ | 10-12. Consequence. (Imprecation.)
| | L⁵ | h⁵ | 13. Sin. (Injustice.)
| | | i⁵ | 14, 15. Consequence. (Penalty.)
| | L⁶ | h⁶ | 16-21. Sin. (Inhumanity.)
| | | i⁶ | 22, 23. Consequence. (Imprecation.)
| | L⁷ | h⁷ | 24-27. Sins of heart. (Covetousness, 24, 25. Idolatry, 26, 27.)
| | | i⁷ | 28. Consequence. (Penalty.)
| | L⁸ | h⁸ | 29-34. Sins of heart. (Malignity, 29-31. Inhospitality, 32. Hypocrisy, 33, 34).
| | | i⁸ | 35-37. Consequence. (Trial desired.)
| | L⁹ | h⁹ | 38, 39. Sin. (Fraud.)
| | | i⁹ | 40. Consequence.

G. (page 147) chap. xxxi.   *Solemn asseveration of his innocence,
in respect to various sins.*

G

L^1 | h^1 | 1. Sin. (Unchastity.)
i^1 | 2-4. Consequence.

L^2 | h^2 | 5. Sin. (Deceit.)
i^2 | 6. Consequence. (Trial desired.)

L^3 | h^3 | 7. Sin. (Dishonesty.)
i^3 | 8. Consequence. (Imprecation.)

L^4 | h^4 | 9. Sin. (Adultery.)
i^4 | 10-12. Consequence. (Imprecation.)

L^5 | h^5 | 13. Sin. (Injustice.)
i^5 | 14, 15. Consequence. (Penalty.)

L^6 | h^6 | 16-21. Sin. (Inhumanity.)
i^6 | 22, 23. Consequence. (Imprecation.)

L^7 | h^7 | 24-27. Sins of heart. (Covetousness, 24, 25. Idolatry, 26, 27.)
i^7 | 28. Consequence. (Penalty.)

L^8 | h^8 | 29-34. Sins of heart. (Malignity, 29-31. Inhospitality, 32. Hypocrisy, 33, 34).
i^8 | 35-37. Consequence. (Trial desired.)

L^9 | h^9 | 38, 39. Sin. (Fraud.)
i^9 | 40. Consequence.

G. (page 155) chap. xxxi. *Job's solemn asseveration of his innocence, in respect to various sins.*

L¹ (page 155) chap. xxxi. 1-4. *Unchastity.*

1. A covenant for[1] mine eyes I made [with God];
   How then could I upon a virgin gaze?
2. What would my judgment be from ᴳᴼᴰ[2] above?
   Or what my lot from Shaddai on high?
3. Is not calamity for evil men?
   To those who sin is not disaster[3] due?
4. Would not Eloah[4] see my [evil] way?
   [Would He not] take account of all my steps?

L² (page 155) chap. xxxi. 5, 6. *Deceit.*

5. If I have walked in ways of falsity,
   Or, If my foot had hasted to deceit
6. Then let Him weigh me in just balances,
   And let Eloah know my blamelessness.

L³ (page 155) chap. xxxi. 7, 8. *Dishonesty.*

7. If, from THE way, my step aside hath swerved;
   And I have coveted[5] what I had seen;
   Or, any stain has cleaved unto my hands,
8. Then let me sow, and let another reap[6]
   And let my plantings[7] all be rooted up.

---

[1] Not "made with," for that would require םִע *(im)*. The covenant here was made with God, against his eyes, which are regarded as an enemy likely to lead him astray.

[2] Heb., *Ĕloah.*

[3] Heb., *strange* punishment.

[4] Heb., *He.*

[5] Heb., "Or, if my heart had followèd mine eyes." By the Figure *Prosopopœia* the heart is personified; and by *Synecdoche* it (as a part) is put for the whole person. By *Metonymy* (of the cause) it is also put for the *desires* of the heart; and by *Metonymy* also the *eyes* are put for that which is seen by the eyes.

[6] Heb., *eat.*

[7] Heb., *produce:* or, that which is growing up: *i.e.*, that which has been planted stands in contrast with its being rooted up.

L ¹ (page 155) chap. xxxi. 9-12.   *Adultery.*

9. By woman, if my heart has been enticed,
    And at my neighbour's door I have laid wait ;
10. Then let my wife grind [corn]¹ for other men,
    Let others humble her [as if their slave].
11. For such a deed ² would be a heinous sin,
    A sin that must be brought before the judge.³
12. It is a fire that to Abaddon burns,
    Destroying ⁴ all my increase at the root.

L ⁵ (page 155) chap. xxxi. 13-15.   *Injustice.*

13. If I had spurned my servants' ⁵ righteous cause,
    When they had brought before me their complaint.
14. What then could I have done when GOD ⁶ rose up ?
    When He required, what could I answer Him ?
15. Who in the womb made ME; made He not HIM ?
    And from one source gave being to us both ?

L ⁶ (page 155) chap. xxxi. 16-23.   *Inhumanity.*

16. If from the poor man's prayer ⁷ I turned away ⁸
    [Or, If] I caused the widow's eyes to fail ⁹

---

¹ Compare Ex. xi. 5. Judg. xvi. 21. Lam. v. 13. Isa. xlvii. 2. Matt. xxiv. 41.

² Heb., הִיא (*hē*) *this* : *i.e.*, this sin of adultery.

³ Heb., *a sin for the judges*. Some Codices with two early printed editions read, *a judicial iniquity*. In some Codices the Massorah says, "read judicial." The meaning is the same as when we speak of a thing being " a crime in the eye of the law :" Or, an " indictable offence." Compare *v.* 28.

⁴ Preserving and combining the two ideas suggested by *fire* and *Abaddon*. The latter means *destruction*, and fire *destroys* by burning. *Uprooting* is out of all harmony with the scope of the passage.

⁵ Heb., *man - servant and maid-servant*.

⁶ Heb., *El*.

⁷ Heb., *desire*.

⁸ Heb., *witheld* or *kept aloof*, the subjective future implying *disposition* rather than act.

⁹ *i.e.*, with looking in vain for help. Comp. Lam. iv. 17.

17. And eaten my [sweet] morsel all alone,
    So that the fatherless ate not thereof ?
18. [But no !]. As with a father he grew up
    With me. And from my birth [2] I guided her [3]
19. If e'er I saw one perishing [with cold] [4]
    Or any needy without covering,
20. Has not His [very] loins,[5] me blessed [6] indeed,
    When he has felt the warmth of my lambs' fleece,
21. If 'gainst the orphan I have raised my hand,
    Because I saw the Judge [7] would take my part,[8]
22. [Then] let my shoulder [9] fall from out its blade,
    And [let] my arm [10] be broken from its bone.
23. For GOD'S [11] destruction would have been my dread,
    Before His Majesty I could not stand.

L[7] (page 155) chap. xxxi. 24-28. *Sins of heart. Covetousness*
(*vv.* 24, 25).

24. If I have put my confidence in gold,
    Or, to the fine gold said [' Thou art] my trust ; '
25. If I rejoiced because my wealth was great,
    Because my hand [12] had vast abundance gained,

Idolatry (*vv.* 26, 27).

26. If on the sun I looked as it shone forth,
    Or, on the moon, so bright, as it marched on,

---

[1] Heb., *grew up from my youth* (*i.e.,* the orphan).

[2] Heb., *from the womb of my mother*.

[3] *i.e.,* the widow.

[4] Heb., *without clothing*.

[5] Written *sing.* but read dual. In some Codices, with three early printed editions, both written and read " loins " (dual). See Ginsburg's Text and note.

[6] By *Prosopopœia* the loins are personified.

[7] Heb., *at the gate* : *i.e.,* the judge sitting in the gate.

[8] Heb., *my help* : put by *Metonymy* (of the adjunct) for one who would help me, be on my side, or take my part.

[9] The upper bone of the arm.

[10] The lower bone of the arm.

[11] Heb., *El*.

[12] By *Synecdoche, my hand,* is put for *myself,* denoting how the wealth had acquired : viz., by his own labour.

27. And my heart had been secretly enticed,
    So that my hand [in worship] touched my mouth [1]
28. This, too, had been a sin before the Law [2]
    For then I had denied the GOD [3] above.

L [8] (page 155) chap. **xxxi.** 19-37. *Sins of Heart. Malignity*
                    (*vv.* 29-30).

29. If in my foe's misfortune I rejoiced,
    Or did exult [4] when evil came on him ;
30. (But no! I suffered not my mouth to sin,
    By asking for a curse upon his soul [5]).
31. Though, have not those of mine own household said,
    Oh! that we had [our enemy's] flesh [to eat],
    That we could satiate ourselves [therewith] ?

Inhospitality (v. 32).

32. The stranger never lodged outside [my tent] ;
    My doors I opened to the traveller.

Hypocrisy (vv. 33, 34).

33. If I, like Adam, my transgression [6] hid,
    And in my breast concealed my secret sin,
34. Then let me tremble at the rabble crowd,
    Yea, let the scorn of men of rank,[7] affright,
    And let me silence keep, and go not forth.

---

[1] This act of touching the mouth with the hand is put by *Metonymy* (of the Adjunct) for the adoration and worship connected with the act.

[2] See note on verse 11.

[3] Heb., *El.*

[4] Heb., *lift myself up.*

[5] *i.e., himself.*

[6] So (sing.) some codices with two early printed editions, and the Sept. and Vulg. Versions. See Ginsburg's Text and Note.

[7] Heb., *families ;* put by *Metonymy* (of adjunct), for men of good family.

35. (Oh ! that there were for me[1] one who would hear
    What I've marked down![2] Let Shaddai answer me !
    Or, let mine Adversary write[3] HIS charge!
36. Would I not on my shoulder lift it up,
    Or bind it, as a crown, upon [my head]?
37. The number of my steps[4] I would declare
    Yea, as a prince I would draw near to him).

L[9] (page 155) chap. xxxi. 38-40.   *Fraud.*

38. If, the whole Land, against me had cried out,
    And [if] its furrows, all together wept,[5]
39. If, without having paid I ate its fruits,
    And thus have made its owners breathe out [hate][6]
40. [Then] let there come forth thorns[7] instead of wheat,
    And noxious weeds, instead of barley, grow.

Job's words are ended:[8] [he will say no more]

---

[1] Heb., *That I had.*

[2] Heb., *my mark: i.e.*, what I have marked or noted down. Compare ch. xiii. 18 ; xxiii. 4, and Ezek. ix. 4.

[3] The writing that Job desired could have been only the indictment against him ; or the evidence as to its counts or charges.

It might be rendered, Let the writing answer me which mine Adversary hath written.

[4] *i.e.*, I would go boldly forward to meet my Adversary, and not, like Adam (*v.* 33), hide myself.

[5] The Figure *Prosopopœia* by which the furrows are personified.

[6] Heb., *caused to breathe out* (or *expire*) *the soul of its owners: i.e.*, caused them to die of hunger by fraudulently consuming the fruits of their toil without payment.

[7] Heb., *the thorn.*

[8] This is not a mere epigraph of a writer, or editor. They are the concluding words which Job uttered; by which he informed his friends that he did not intend to carry the controversy any further; but that he had now said all he meant to say. So far as he was concerned, the controversy was ended.

THE MINISTRY OF ELIHU

E. (page 54) chap. xxxii. 1—xxxvii. 33.

E | Y | xxxii. 1-5. Connecting Narrative. (Prose.)
| Z | xxxii. 6—xxxvii. 33. The Ministry Proper. (Poetry.)

Y. (above) chap. xxxii. 1-6. *Connecting narrative.*

Y | a | xxxii. 1. Three men. Cessation.
     b | 2, 3. Anger of Elihu.
    a | 4. One man. Forbearance.
     b | 5. Anger of Elihu.

Connecting Narrative.

a | 1. So these three men ceased to answer Job because he was righteous in their [1] eyes.

  b | 2, 3. Then was kindled the anger of Elihu [2] son of Barachel [3] the Buzite [4] of the family of Ram.[5] Against Job was kindled his anger, because he justified himself [6] rather than God.[7] Also against his three friends was his anger kindled, because they had found no answer, and had condemned God.[8]

a | 4. Now Elihu had wanted to speak concerning Job,[9] because they [10] were older [11] than he.

  b | 5. Howbeit, when Elihu saw that there was no answer in the mouth of the three men, then his anger was kindled.

---

[1] So it should be, according to the Septuagint. See Ginsburg's Introduction p. 361. Their cessation was caused by their conviction that Job was righteous ; whereas, as long as they thought otherwise they did not cease.

[2] *My God is He.*

[3] *Blessing of God.*

[4] *Contempt.*

[5] Buz was the second son of Nahor. See Gen. xxii. 21. So that Elihu was the son of Barachel ; Barachel was of the tribe of Buz (a "Buzite") ; and of the family of Ram. (Not the Aram of that verse, as Barachel could not be descended from both the second and third sons of Nahor.

Elihu was therefore a descendant

ELIHU'S MINISTRY PROPER.

Z. (page 161) chaps. xxxii.—xxxvii. 33.

Z | A¹ | xxxii. 6-22.   Elihu.   Introduction.
        B¹ | xxxiii. 1-33.   His words to Job.

     A² | xxxiv. 1.   Elihu.   Continuation.
        B² | xxxiv. 2-37.   His words to Job's friends.

     A³ | xxxv. 1.   Elihu.   Continuation.
        B³ | xxxv. 2-16.   His words to Job.

     A⁴ | xxxvi. 1.   Elihu.   Conclusion.
        B⁴ | xxxvi. 2—xxxvii. 24.   His words on God's behalf.

A ¹. (above) chap. xxxii. 6-22.   *Elihu (Introduction).*

A¹ | c | 6-.   Personal.   Seniority.
        d | -6, 7.   Reason for not speaking before.
     c | 8, 9.   Personal.   Qualification.
        d | 10-22.   Reason for speaking now.

---

of Nahor, the brother of Abram.
See further on ch. i. 1.

⁶ Heb., *his own soul.*

⁷ See ch. iv. 17, and compare
xxxiii. 9 ; xxxiv. 5 ; xxxv. 2.

⁸ *Elohim* (God) was the primitive
reading here, which is one of the
emendations made by the *Sopherim*

(see note on chap. i. 5).   They
altered אֱלֹהִים (*Elohim*) to אִיּוֹב (*Job*),
out of a mistaken reverence for God.
(See Ginsburg's *Introduction* p. 361.

⁹ Heb., *had waited with words :   i.e.,*
waited to utter his words, or, *to speak.*

¹⁰ *i.e.,* the Three Friends.

¹¹ Heb., *older in days.*

A [1]. (page 162) chap. xxxii. 6-22. *Elihu. (Introduction.)*

6. So then, Elihu, the son of Barachel the Buzite opened his discourse [1] and said :—

c. (page 162) chap. xxxii. 6-. *Personal. (Juniority.)*

I am but young in years,[2] and ye are old,

d. (page 162) chap. xxxi. -6. *Reason for not speaking before.*

Wherefore it was that I held back in fear,
And durst not show what my opinion was.
7. For those of many days should speak, I thought,
A multitude of years should wisdom teach.

c. (page 162) chap. xxxii. 8, 9. *Personal. (Qualifications.)*

8. Surely a spirit dwells in mortal man,
And Shaddai's breath makes them to understand
9. The greatest men are not at all times wise ;
Nor do the aged [always] know what's right.

d. (page 162) chap. xxxii. 10-22. *Reason for speaking now.*

10. Therefore I said, Oh Hearken unto me,
I too will show my knowledge, even I.
11. Lo ! I have listened unto your discourse ;
To all your reas'nings, I have given ear,
Waiting till ye have searched out what to say.
12. But, though to you I carefully gave heed,
There was not one of you convincèd Job ; [3]
Not one who really answered what he said.

---

[1] See note on chap. iii. 1.   [2] Heb., *days.*
[3] See chap. xxxi. 35, 36.

13. I pray you, say not ' We have wisdom found,' [1]
    For God alone can put him right,[2] not man.
14. Since not 'gainst ME hath he arrayed his words ;
    I will not, with YOUR words, reply to him.
15. (All broken down, they answer him no more.
    They have not any more, a word to say,
16. And still I waited, though they could not speak ;
    But silent stood and offered no reply.)
17. I will reply—ev'n I—on mine own part
    I too will show my knowledge, even I.
18. For I am fillèd full with [wisdom's] words ;
    The spirit in my breast [3] constraineth me.
19. It [3] is as wine which hath no safety vent ;
    Like wine-skins new, which are about to burst.
20. Yes, I will speak, that I may find relief ;
    Open my lips, and take up my discourse.
21. I will not now regard the face of man,
    And, to no man, will flattering titles give.
22. I know not how to flatter.[4]   Otherwise
    My Maker soon would summon me away.

---

[1] Compare xxviii. 12, 20, 21 ; xv. 2, 3, 8 ; xii. 2 ; xiii. 2 ; *i.e.*, we have discovered the truth as to Job, that he has richly deserved all his troubles.

[2] Heb., *drive* or *chase away* as chaff by the wind. Ps. i. 4 ; lxviii. 3, *put him to flight* would be a good rendering ; but, what sort of flight, must be determined by the previous line, and the context.

[3] Heb., *my belly* : "belly" being put by *Metonymy* for the seat of feeling and thought, must be rendered by words suitable to English usage.

[4] Heb., *give flattering titles.*

B¹. (page 162) chap. xxxiii. 1-33. *Elihu's words to Job.*

B¹ | C | e¹ | 1, 2. **Call for attention.**

        f¹ | 3, 4. **His fitness.** { g | 3. Internal.
                                          h | 4. External.

    e² | 5. **Call for answer.**

        f² | 6, 7. **His fitness.** { h | 6. External.
                                          g | 7. Internal.

          D | i | 8-11. Job's error. Justification of himself.

                k | 12. Answer. God's greatness (in Creation).

        D | i | 13. Job's error. Charge against God.

              k | 14-30. Answer. God's goodness (in Revelation).

C | e³ | 31-. **Call for silence.**

        f³ | -31. **His fitness.** " I will speak."

    e⁴ | 32. **Call for answer.**

        f⁴ | 33. **His fitness.** " I will teach."

---

e¹ (above) chap. xxxiii. 1, 2. *Call for attention.*

xxxiii. 1. And now, O Job, I pray thee hear me speak,
    And be attentive to my every word.
  2. Behold now, I have openèd my mouth ;
    My tongue shall utt'rance [1] give, distinct and clear:

---

[1] Heb., *my tongue hath spoken in my palate :* i.e., as my palate discerns the different tastes of foods, so can my tongue discern what words to say. The figure transfers the sense to mental discernment, as the tongue is the same agent in each case.

f¹ (page 165) chap. xxxiii. 3, 4. *His fitness.*

3. For all that I shall say comes from my heart,
My lips shall speak what is sincere and true.
God's Spirit made me [at the first] and [still]
4. 'Tis the Almighty's breath must quicken me.¹

e² (page 165) chap. xxxiii. 5. *Call for answer.*

5. If thou art able ; answer me, I pray :
Array thy words in order ; take thy stand.

f² (page 165) chap. xxxiii. 6, 7. *His fitness.*

6. Lo, I am here—thou wished it ²—in GOD's stead.
And of the clay I have been formed [like thee].
7. Behold, my terror will not make thee fear ;
Nor heavy will my hand³ upon thee press.

i. (page 165) chap. xxxiii. 8-11. *Job's error. Justification of himself.*

8. But, surely, thou hast spoken in mine ears,
And I have heard a voice of words, like these ⁴
9.   ' A man without transgression, pure am I :
       ' Yea, I am clean ; without iniquity.
10.   ' He is against me ; seeking ⁵ grounds of strife ;
       ' And He doth count ⁶ me as His enemy,⁷
11.   ' My feet He setteth fast within the stocks,
       ' And taketh observation of my ways.

---

¹ Referring to Gen. ii. 7.
² See chap. xiii. 3, 18-24, &c. ; xvi. 21 ; xxiii., 3-9 ; xxx. 20 ; xxxi. 35.
³ So it should be, with Sept. See Ginsburg's Text and note.
⁴ See chap. ix. 17 ; x. 7 ; xi. 4 ; xvi. 17 ; xxiii., 10-11 ; xxvii. 5 ; xxix. 14 ; and xxxi. 1.

⁵ See the word and its root, תְּנוּאוֹת *(tenūōth).* Num. xiv. 35 ; xxxii. 7.
⁶ Some Codices, with one early printed Edition, Sept., Syriac, and Vulgate, so read it. See Ginsburg's Text and note.
⁷ Heb., *for an enemy to him.*

k. (page 165) chap. xxxiii. 12.   *Answer.   God's greatness (in creation).*

12. Behold, thou art not just : I answer thee,
   HOW GREAT IS G⦿D[1] COMPARED WITH
   MORTAL MAN.[2]

i. (page 165) chap. xxxiii. 13.   *Job's Error.   Charge against God.*

13. Why, then, against Him didst thou dare complain.
   That by no word of His, He answ'reth [3] thee ?

---

k. (page 165) chap. xxxiii. 14-30.   *God's goodness (in Revelation).*

k | 1[1] | 14, 15. Means. (Dreams and Visions.)
   | | m[1] | 16-18. Ends. (Neg.)
   | 1[2] | 19-22. Means. (Afflictions.)
   | | m[2] | 23-28. Ends. (Pos.)
  } In detail.

   | 1[3] | 29. Means. (All these means.)
   | | m[3] | 30. Ends. (Neg. 30-. Pos. -30.)
  } In sum.

1[1] (above) chap. xxxiii. 14, 15.   *Means.   In detail.*
   (*Dream and Visions.*)

14. For GOD [4] DOTH speak. He speaks in sundry ways :
   Again, again,[5] though man regard it not.

---

1 Heb., Eloah.
2 Heb., *mortal man.* See note on chap. iv. 17.
3 As in Isa. xxxvi. 2 ; Jer. xlii. 4 ; xlv. 20. See A.V. margin.
4 Heb., *El.*
5 Heb., *once, twice.* This is the idiom for more than once : *i.e.*, *repeatedly*, or as we have rendered it in English idiom, *again, again.* See *v.* 29 ; ch. xl. 5. Ps. lxii. 11, and compare 2 Kings vi. 10 and the same Heb., idiom carried into the N.T. Phil. iv. 16, and 1 Thess. ii. 18.

15. He speaks in dreams, and visions of the night [1]
     When, deep in slumber, lying on their bed,
     There falls on men an overwhelming sleep.

m [1] (page 167) chap. xxxiii. 16-18. *Ends.*

16. Then opens He their ear, that they may hear,
     Pressing, as with a seal, the warning given.[2]
17. To make [3] a man withdraw himself from sin ;
     Or keep him [4] from the [dangerous [5]] way of pride.
18. Back from the pit 'tis thus He keeps a man ;
     And saves his life from falling by the sword.

l [2] (page 167) chap. xxxiii. 19-22. *Means. In detail. (Afflictions.)*

19. He speaks again,[6] when, chastened, on his bed [7]
     Another lies, his bones all racked with pain ;
20. So that his daily food he doth abhor ;
     And turns against his choicest [8] dainty meat
21. His flesh, it wastes away,[9] and is not seen :
     His bones, before concealed, show through his skin.
22. Unto destruction he is drawing nigh ;
     And death's dark angel [10] waits to end his life.

---

[1] Compare Gen. xx. 3. Dan. iv. 5. Some Codices read " in a vision," with Sept., Syr. and Vulg. See Ginsburg's Text and note.

[2] Pressing on the mind by the Dream or Vision the warning thus conveyed, as an impression is made with a seal on wax or clay.

[3] The Hiphil here is intensive. The Syr. and Vulg., read "from his sin." See Ginsburg's Text and note.

[4] Heb., *to hide*, or *conceal: i.e.*, so that man should not see, and thus be kept from the danger.

[5] Some such word seems to be required to show the real nature of pride, (compare Prov. vi. 16, 17 ; xvi. 5. 1 Tim. iii. 6). Pride ever goes before a fall and hence its danger.

[6] This is another way in which God speaks to man.

[7] 2 Kings xx. 1, 3, 5, 12-19. 2 Chron. xxxii. 24-26, 31.

[8] Or, *once-loved.* Heb., *food of desire.*

[9] Heb., *wasteth from sight.*

[10] Heb., *the making to die : i.e.*, whatever the disease may be which is destroying his life. We have used a Figurative expression to denote these messengers of death. That this figure is Scriptural may be seen from 1 Chron. xxi. 15. Ps. lxxviii. 49. Compare Lu. xii. 20.

m² (page 167) chap. xxxiii. 23-28.   *Ends (Positive.)*

23. Then, then, He speaks with him ¹ by Messenger
     Who can interpret : ² —One, 'mong thousands chief,
     Who will reveal to man HIS ³ righteousness.
24. Then He doth show him grace [Divine, and saith] : —
     ' Deliver him from going down to death ;
     ' A Ransom I have found—Redemption's price.'
25. Young, as a child's, becomes his flesh again,
     And to his youthful days he doth return.
26. He, supplication makes to Eloah,
     Who grace and favour showeth unto him,'⁴
     So that he looks up to God's ⁵ face with joy.⁶
     Thus, [He] doth give to man HIS righteousness.
27. This, then, becomes the burden of his song : ⁷
     ' I sinned ! and I perverted what was right,
     ' Although no profit from it came to me.
28.   ' My ⁸ soul HE hath redeemèd from the pit ;
     ' My ⁹ life shall yet again behold the light.

---

¹ Another way by which God speaks to man.

² Or *interpreter : i.e.,* one who can interpret and reveal the truth concerning God and His ways. This is the meaning of John i. 18.

³ *i.e.,* God's righteousness.

⁴ Heb., *accepteth him.* Ch. xxii. 27.

⁵ Heb., *His.*

⁶ Heb., *shout of joy : i.e., joyful* shouts.

⁷ These are the joyful shouts, and what he sings is the evidence of his possession now of Divine and heavenly "wisdom" and "understanding."

⁸ Written "my," but to be read "his." In some codices, with four early printed Editions, Sept., and Syr., "my" is both written and read. But in others, with one early printed Edition, Aramaic and Vulg., "his" is both written and read. See Ginsburg's Heb. Text and note. If "my" is correct, then it is the man's joyful shout ; but if "his" is correct, then it is what Elihu says, and should not be indented.

⁹ Written "my" but to be read "his." In some codices, with one early printed Edition, and Sept., "my" is both written and read. But in others, with five early printed Editions, and Aramaic, "his" is both written and read. See Ginsburg's Text and note. See end of note above.

l³ (page 167) chap. xxxiii. 29.   *Means (in sum).*

29. Thus doth God speak, in all these sundry ways:
Time after time;¹ and yet again He speaks:

m³ (page 167) chap. xxxiii. 30),   *Ends (neg. and pos.)*

30. That from destruction He may save a soul,²
And make him joy in light—the light of life.³

e³ (page 167) chap. xxxiii. 31-.   *Call for silence.*

31. Mark this, O Job; and hearken unto me.

f ³ (page 167) chap. xxxiii. -31.   *His fitness.*

I will now speak: and as for thee, hold thou
Thy peace; while I, with words of wisdom, teach.

e⁴ (page 167) chap. xxxiii. 32.   *Call for answer.*

32. If there is any answer, answer me.
Speak: for I long to see thee justified.

f⁴ (page 167) chap. xxxiii. 33.   *His fitness.*

33. If not; do thou then hearken unto me:
Hold thou thy peace, while wisdom I impart.

---

¹ Heb., פַּעֲמַיִם (paamayim) *two strokes*, or *two ways*. The Heb., idiom is thus, "*two ways, three*": *i.e.*, repeatedly. See note on *v.* 14.

² The Heb. idiom for *him* or *himself*.

³ See above, *v.* 28; iii. 16. Ps. xlix. 9; lvi. 13.

B ². (page 162) chap. xxxiv. 2-37.   *Elihu's words to Job's friends.*

B² | E | n | 2-4.   Appeal to his hearers.

             o | 5, 6.   Job's error.   (5, Himself.   5, 6, God.)

                p | 7-9.   His reproof.

                    F | q | 10-.   Call for attention.

                           r | -10-15.   Vindication of God.

                  F | *q* | 16.   Call for attention.

                           r | 17-33-.   Vindication of God.

    E | *n* | -33, 34.   Appeal to his hearers.

            o | 35.   Job's error.

              p | 36, 37.   His reproof.

---

n. (above) chap. xxxiv. 1-4.   *Elihu's appeal to his hearers.*

1. Furthermore, Elihu addressed [1] [Job's friends] and said :
2. Hear now my words ye wise [and knowing] [2] men;
   And ye who knowledge have, give ear to me.
3. For 'tis the ear that [proves and] trieth speech,
   Ev'n as the palate shows what's good to eat.
4. Then, let us, what is right, choose [3] for ourselves :
   And let us know, between us, what is good.

---

[1] See note on chap. iv. 1.

[2] Compare *v.* 10.

[3] Heb., בָּחַר (*bachar*), *to examine*, but with a view to making a **choice.**
So 1 Thess. v. 20.

o. (page 171) chap. **xxxiv. 5, 6.** *Job's Error.*

5. Now Job hath said—

'I have been [and am] just:
'But GOD [1] my righteous cause hath turned away. [2]

6. 'Against my right shall I speak what is false?
'Sore is my wound; [3] though, through no sin of mine.

p. (page 171) chap. **xxxiv. 7-9.** *Reproof.*

7. Where is the worthy [4] man [who] like to Job,
Drinks up as water all your scornful words?

8. And keepeth company with those who sin,
And keepeth company with wicked men?

9. For he hath said

'It profiteth not man
'That he should take delight in Elohim.' [5]

q (page 171) xxxiv. **10-.** *Call for attention.*

10-. To this, ye wise men, list to my reply:

r (page 171) xxxiv. **-10-15.** *Vindication of God.*

-10. Far be such evil from the mighty GOD, [6]
And such iniquity from Shaddai.

11. For sure, man's work He will repay to him,
And will requite according to his ways.

12. Nay, surely, GOD [6] will not do wickedly,
And Shaddai will not pervert the right.

13. Who unto him did delegate the charge
Of Earth? Or trusted Him with all the World?

---

[1] Heb., *El.*
[2] Heb., *caused to be put aside.*
[3] Heb., *mine arrow*: put by *Metonymy* (of cause) for the wound caused by it.
[4] Heb., גֶּבֶר (gever) *mighty man.*

See note on chap. iv. 17.
[5] See ch. ix. 22 &c.; xxi. 7 &c.; xxiv. 1 &c. He himself admitted that such speeches were wrong, though he did not cease from them.
[6] Heb., *El.*

14. Should He think only of Himself,[1] [and all]
His breath, yea breath of life [2] withdraw,

15. All flesh together would [at once] expire,
The noblest man [3] would unto dust return.

q. (page 171) **xxxiv.** 16. *Call for attentiou.*

16. Now, if thou understanding hast, Hear this,
Give heed unto the teaching [5] of my words.

i. (page 171) chap. xxxiv. 17-33-). *Vindication of God.*

17. Can one who hateth justice rule [the World]?
Wilt thou condemn the Just, the Mighty One?

18. Shall one say to a King—'Thou worthless man'?
Or, unto nobles say, 'Ye wicked men'?

19. How much less, then, wilt thou say it to Him?
Who [neither] doth accept the face [6] of kings,
Nor doth regard the rich above [7] the poor,
For they are all the work of His own hands,

20. They, in a moment, die, ev'n in a night; [8]
The people tremble when they pass away:
The mighty fall,[9] but by no [human] hand.[10]

21. For His eyes are upon the ways of men,[11]
And all his footsteps He doth see [and note].

---

1 Heb., *set his heart on himself.*

2 Heb., *breath and spirit* is the figure *Hendiadys = His breath—yes, His spirit I mean.*

3 Heb., אִישׁ (*îsh*), see note on ch. iv. 17.

4 Gen. ii. 7; iii. 19. Ecc. xii. 7. Ps. civ. 29.

5 See the Oxford Gesenius 877, 3, *a* (1).

6 *i.e., persons:* the *face* being put by *Synecdoche* for the *person:* a part for the whole.

7 Heb., *before.*

8 Heb., *midnight.*

9 Heb., *are caused to be taken away;. i.e.,* are deposed.

10 Heb., *without hand.* See Dan. ii 34, 45; viii. 25. Lam. iv. 6 : *i.e., without* human *hand,* meaning that he is smitten by the hand of God. Compare 1 Sam. xxvi. 10. 2 Sam. xxiv. 16.

11 Heb., *a man.*

22. There is no darkness, and no shade of death,
    Where workers of iniquity may hide.
23. Man[1] doth not need repeated scrutiny,
    When he to GOD[2] in [final] judgment comes.
24. He breaks the strong in ways we cannot trace ;[3]
    And others, in their stead, He setteth up.
25. That's why[4] he taketh knowledge of their works,
    And, in a night, he overthroweth them
    [In such a way] that, they are [all] destroyed.
26. [Sometimes][5] He smites the wicked where they stand[6]
    In open sight of all men who behold[7]
27. Because they turned away from following Him,
    And would not have regard to all His ways;[8]
28. But [by oppression] brought[9] the poor man's cry
    To Him, Who hears the plaint of the oppressed.
29. When he gives quiet, Who can e'er disturb ?
    Or, Who can see Him when He hides His face?
    (Whether it be a nation or a man ?
30. Whether because the godless may not reign,
    Or, those who of the people make a prey.[10])
31. If Job had [spoken[11]] unto God,[2] [and] said :
    ' I have borne chastisement : and never more
32. ' Will I transgress ; That which I do not see
    ' Teach me Thyself.   If in the past I wrought
    ' Iniquity, I will not work it more :'
33. Shall He requite on thine own terms,[12] [and say]
    ' As thou wilt choose[13] [so be it] not as I ?

---

[1] Heb., *he.*

[2] Heb., *El.*

[3] Heb., *unsearchable : i.e., past finding out.*

[4] Heb., *therefore*, or *to this end.*

[5] This is another case which is not inscrutable ; but visible to all.

[6] Compare ch. xl. 12.

[7] Heb., *in the place of beholders.*

[8] *i.e., any of His ways.*

[9] Heb., *cause to reach.*

[10] Heb., *from snares of the people : i.e.,* who *ensnare*, and thus make a prey of the people.

[11] Heb., [what] *to be said : i.e., it is meet to be said.*

[12] Heb., *that which is from thee.*

[13] Heb.,*as thou rejectest or choosest.*

n. (page 171) chap. xxxiv. -33, 34). *Appeal to his hearers.*

-33. Say therefore, now, O Job, if thou dost know.

34. For ME, would men of understanding speak; [1]
　Yea, every wise man listening now [will say],

　　o. (page 171) chap. xxxiv. 35. *Job's reproof.*

35.　'Job, without knowledge, spoke in ignorance,
　　'And without understanding were his words.[2] '

36. Oh, would that Job were proved unto the end,[3]
　For his replies are those of evil men.

37. Rebellion he doth add unto his sin ;
　'Mong US, he, in defiance, claps his hands,
　And against GOD, [4] he multiplies his words.

B[3]. (page 162) chap. xxxv. 2-16. *Elihu's words to Job.*

B [3] | G [1] | s [1] | 2, 3. Job's error. ⎱
　　　　　　　　 t [1] | 4-8.　Answer.　 ⎰ Personal.

　　　 G [2] | s [2] | 9.　Men's error. ⎱
　　　　　　　　 t [2] | 10-13. Answer. ⎰ General.

　　　 G [3] | s [2] | 14-.　Job's error. ⎱
　　　　　　　　 t [3] | -14-16. Answer. ⎰ Personal.

---

[1] *i.e.,* I need not say it myself.
Every sensible man may well say it
for me.

[2] So. ch. xxxv. 16.
[3] See Oxford Gesenius, 664ᴬ , 3.
[4] Heb., *El.*

s ¹. (page 175) chap. xxxv. 1-3. *Job's error. (Personal.)*

1. Elihu then addressed¹ [Job] and said
2. Dost thou count this sound judgment ? Thou didst say,
   ' My righteousness surpasseth that of GOD ; ' ²
3. Yea—thou dost ask ' What is the gain to thee ? '
   And, ' Shall I profit more than by my sin ? '

t ¹. (page 175) chap. xxxv. 4-8. *Elihu's answer.*

4. I—even I, will make reply³ to thee,
   And, with thee, to these friends⁴ of thine as well :—
5. Look up unto the heav'ns ; Consider them ;
   Survey the skies, so high above thy head.
6. If thou hast sinned, What doèst thou to Him ? ⁵
   Be thy sins many, What dost thou to Him ?
7. If thou art just, What dost thou give to Him ?
   Or from thy hand what [gift] will He receive ?
8. Thy sin may hurt a mortal like thyself ;
   Thy righteousness may profit one like thee.

s ². (page 175) chap. xxxv. 9. *Men's error. (General.)*

9. Men make an outcry when they are oppressed :
   They cry for help when 'neath the tyrant's pow'r ⁶

t ². (page 175) chap. xxxv. 10-13. *Elihu's answer.*

10. But no one saith ' Where is my Maker—GOD ? ' ⁷
    Who giveth songs to us in sorrow's night ; ⁸

---

¹ See note on ch. iv. 1.

² Heb., *El.*

³ Heb., *return thee words ;* or, *with words : i.e.,* plain and clear.

⁴ Heb., *companions,* or *friends.* Comp. ch. xxxii. 1, 3.

⁵ Or, *How can that affect Him ?*

⁶ *Heb., arm,* which is put **by** Metonymy for *power.*

⁷Heb., *Eloah.*

⁸ Heb., *in the night:* or *the night-time ;* put by *Metonymy* (of **the** Adjunct) for trouble which so often comes in the night, and is **thus** associated with it.

11. And teacheth us beyond the beasts of earth,
    And makes us wiser than the fowl of heaven ?
12. But, why[1] He answers not, though men may cry,
    Is the o'erweening pride of evil doers.
13. For, vanity, GOD[2] will in no wise hear,[3]
    Nor will th' Almighty[4] hold it in regard.

s[3]. (page 175) xxxv. 14-. *Job's error.* (*Personal*).

14-. How much less, then, when thou dost say to Him
     'I see Him not : [He doth not hear my cry']

t[3]. (page 175) xxxv. -14-16. *Elihu's answer.*

-14. Yet,—judgment is before Him :[5] therefore, wait.
15. But now, because He hath not punishèd,[6]
    ' [Thou say'st] His anger doth not visit sin ;
    'Nor strictly mark wide-spread[7] iniquity.'
16. Thus Job doth fill His mouth with vanity ;
    And, without knowledge, multiplieth words.

---

[1] The Heb., שָׁם (*shām*) *there* ; may refer to condition as well as to place and time. Compare Ps. cxxxiii. 13, "for *there*: (*i.e.*, in such a condition of things as described) the Lord commanded the blessing."

[2] Heb., *El.*

[3] See chs. xxx. 20 ; xxxi. 35 ; xix 7 ; ix. 16. And compare ch. xii. 4 ; xxiv. i. Ps. xxii. 7, 8 ; xlii. 10, &c.

[4] Heb., *Shaddai.*

[5] Heb., *see Him not* : *i.e.,* **regard** *him not.*

[6] Or, *because it is not* [*so*].

[7] Heb. פּוּשׁ (*pūsh*), *dispersed,* *scattered, spread out.* Used of a stream overflowing. Also of a horse-man prancing proudly Hab. i. 8 ; of calves leaping and sporting Mal. iv. 2 (iii. 20) Jer. l. 11. of a people *scattered* and dispersed Nah. iii. **18.**

B⁴ (page 162) chaps. xxxvi. 2—xxxvii. 24. *Elihu's words on God's behalf.*

B⁴ | G | xxxvi. 2-4. Introduction. " On God's behalf."

     H | u | 5. His attribute. "God is great."

         v | 6-15. Manifested in Providence.

            w | 16-25. Application and Exhortation to fear His wondrous wrath.

     H | u | 26. His attribute. God is great.

         v | 27—xxxvii. 13. Manifested in Creation.

            w | 14-22-. Application and Exhortation to consider His "wondrous works."

   G | -22, 24. Conclusion. On God's behalf.

G. (above) chap. xxxvi. 1-4. *Introduction. " On God's behalf."*

1. Elihu also went on ¹ to say
2. Bear with me ² while I, briefly, make thee see
   That there are words to say on GOD's ³ behalf.
3. My knowledge I shall gather from afar,
   And, to my Maker, righteousness ascribe.
4. Truly, no falsehood in my word shall be :
   Th' Omniscient One ⁴ it is who deals with thee.

---

¹ See note on ch. iv. 1.
² Heb., *wait for me.* Or, *wait a moment;* as though Job were impatient under his words.

³ Heb., *El.*
⁴ Heb., *perfect of knowledge.* From ch. xxxvii. 16 it is clear that God is meant, and not the speaker.

u. (page 178) chap. xxxvi. 5. *God's attribute.*

5. Lo! GOD[1] IS GREAT,—but naught doth He despise:
   In power great, in wisdom great is He.

v. (page 178) chap. xxxvi. 6-15). *His greatness manifested in Providence.*

6. He will not let the wicked ever live:[2]
   But He will right the cause of the oppressed,
7. And not withdraw His eyes from righteous men.
   He seateth them with kings upon the throne,
   He makes them sit in glory[3]; raiseth them
8. On high. And if they be in fetters bound,
   Or, [if] they be held fast in sorrows bonds,
9. [It is] that He may show them what they've done,
   And that their sins have been produced by pride.[4]
10. Thus openeth He their ear, and doth instruct,[5]
    And warn them from iniquity to turn.
11. Then, If they hearken and obey [His voice]
    They in prosperity shall spend their days,
    [And end] their years in peace and pleasantness.
12. If they heed not, they perish by the sword,
    And die[6] not knowing [how it is or why].

---

1 Heb., *El.*

2 Heb., *let the wicked live.* This is the literal meaning of יְחַיֶּה (*yechayeh*). It does not refer so much to his living on in his wickedness in this world, but he shall not *live* in the highest sense of the word. Compare Rom. vi. 23.

3 לָנֶצַח (*lanetzach*) does not necessarily refer to *time*, but to *degree*. It is a superlative of excellence. The scope of these verses is the same as 1 Sam. ii. 8. Ps. cxiii. 7. Lu. i. 52. Compare 1 Sam. xv. 29, excelling in *strength.* 1 Ch. xxix. 11. Is. xxv. 8, *victory.* Lam. iii. 18, *strength.*

4 Heb., *how they have behaved themselves proudly,* or *walked* in pride.

5 Heb., *to instruction.*

6 Heb., *yield their breath.*

13. ['Tis thus] the godless[1] heap up [fearful] wrath : [2]
   [Because] they cry not when He bindeth them.
14. [Wherefore] they[3] die, while yet they're in their youth,
   Their life is spent among polluted ones.[4]
15. Yet He doth save the poor in all his woes,
   And openeth their ear through their distress.

w. (page 178) chap. xxxvi. 16-25. *Application and exhortation to fear God's Wrath.*

16. Thus, in like manner, He would THEE allure,
   And from the mouth of trouble [succour [5] thee],
   Into a pleasant [6] place :—no trouble [7] there—
   Thy table well prepared [8] with richest food.[9]
17. But [if] thou'rt filled with pleadings of the bad,
   Judgment and justice will lay hold on thee.
18. For, there is wrath ; [beware, then,] of its stroke ; [10]
   For, then, a ransom great will not suffice,
19. Nor treasure turn the threatened stroke aside,
   Nor precious ore avail, nor all thy strength.
20. Oh, long not for the night [of death [11]], in which
   [Whole] nations disappear [12] from out their place

---

[1] Heb., *godless in heart.*

[2] *i.e.*, *treasure up the wrath of God* : " *wrath* " being put by *Metonymy* for the *judgment* which is the outcome of it. Compare Rom. ii. 5.

[3] Heb., *their soul dieth.*

[4] Heb., *Sodomites* : *i.e.*, in a modified sense *effeminates.* See the word in De. xxiii. 18. 1 Kings xiv. 24; xv. 12; xxii. 47; and compare Gen. xxxviii. 21, 22.

[5] Or, *draw thee out,* so as to succour. It is a repetition of what is already implied in the word הֵסִית (*hissīth*) from סוּת (*sūth*) *to incite,* either *to* or *from;* and thus either to allure or to impel.

[6] Heb., " *Broad* " put by *Metonymy* for *prosperity.*

[7] Heb., " *Straitness* " put by Metonymy for trouble or distress.

[8] Heb., *set.* Comp. Ps. xxiii. 5.

[9] Heb., *full of fat.* The idiom for food that is *rich* and good.

[10] Heb., שֶׁפֶק (*sephek*) *a blow.* See the verb in Jer. xxxi. 19. Lam. ii. 15. Ezek. xxi. 12.

[11] Num. xxiv. 10. Compare John ix. 4. Ecc. ix. 5.

[12] Heb., *go up,* used of death, in which the spirit goes up and returns to God (Ecc. xii. 7). Hence, disappear in death, exactly expresses the thought.

21. Take heed! regard not[1] thou iniquity ;
    For this[2] thou didst prefer to all thy woes.
22. Behold, GOD[3] is exalted in His pow'r :
    Who can instruction give, like unto Him ?
23. Who is it that assigns[4] to Him His way ?
    Or, Who can say to Him—' Thou doest wrong ' ?
24. Remember, that thou should'st extol His work,
    Which men have contemplated, and have sung.
25. Yea, all have gazed in wonder[5] thereupon ;
    And mortal man beholds it from afar.

u. (page 178) chap. xxxvi. 26.   *God's Attribute.*

26. Lo! GOD[6] IS GREAT,—[greater] than we can know,
    The number of His years past finding out.

v. (page 178) chaps. xxxvi. 27—xxxvii. 13.   *His greatness manifested in Creation.*

27. 'Tis He who draweth up the vapour-clouds ;
    And they distil [from Heaven] in rain and mist.
28. Ev'n that which from the [low'ring] skies[7] doth fall,
    And poureth down on man abundantly.
29. Can any understand the floatings[8] of
    The clouds ?   The thund'rings of His canopy?
30. Behold, He spreadeth out His light thereon,
    Whilst making dark[9] the bottom of the sea.

---

[1] Heb., *look not.* Do not *set thy face* towards it. " Face " being put by *Synecdoche* for the whole person.

[2] *i.e.,* for death (*v.* 20 and compare chap. iii.).

[3] Heb., *El.*

[4] Heb., פָּקַד (*pāchad*) *to visit ;* hence, *to charge, appoint,* or *assign.* Comp. ch. xxxiv. 13. Jer. xv. 3.

[5] Heb., חָזָה (*chāzah*) *to gaze* as rapt in vision. Hence the noun means a prophet who is *a seer.*

[6] Heb., *El.*

[7] Heb., *the heavens,* which is put by *Metonymy* for the clouds and all that is above the earth.

[8] Or, *suspensions.*

[9] Heb., *covering over.*

31. (Yet, 'tis by these, He, judgment executes ;
    By these He giveth food abundantly).
32. He [graspeth] in His hand [1] the lightning flash ;
    And giveth it commandment where to strike.[2]
33. Of this [3] the noise thereof makes quickly known,
    The [frightened] cattle warn us of the storm [4]

xxxvii. 1. That cometh up. Yea my heart quakes at this.
    And [startled] leapeth up from out its place.
2. Hear ye, Oh hear the roaring of His voice,
    The loud reverberations from His mouth ;
3. As under the whole heav'n He sends it forth.
    His lightning to the Earth's extremities
4. [He sends], and after it the thunder roars.
    He thund'reth with His voice of majesty.
    One cannot trace Him, though His voice be heard.
5. GOD'S [5] voice is marvellous when He thundereth.
    Great things He doth : we comprehend them not.
6. For, to the snow, He saith—' Fall thou on Earth : '
    And to the shower,[6] yea, to the flooding [7] rains
7. Which stop the work [8] of man and make it cease [9]
    That all men, of His doing,[10] may take note.
8. Then must the beasts, each to his covert go,
    And in their lairs, must they [perforce] remain.[11]

---

[1] Heb., כַּפָּיִם *(kappayĭm)* *two hands* (Dual) or *both hands.*

[2] The *Hiphil* well expresses the causative nature of the stroke.

[3] *i.e., of this stroke* of lightning.

[4] Heb., *the herds even of the rising* [storm]. The verb " warns " is suggested by both lines : *tell of, report* or *announce,* suggests that the nature of the announcement is as warning.

[5] Heb., *El.*

[6] Heb., *the* (gentle) *shower* of rain (sing.) ; in contrast with the next line.

[7] Heb., *mighty rains* (pl.)

[8] Heb., *hand ;* put by *Metonymy* for *the work* done by the hand.

[9] Heb., *sealeth up : i.e.,* the sudden storm stops man's work, and shuts him up at home.

[10] So it should be, with the Aramaic version. See Ginsburg's Text and note.

[11] Compare Ps. civ. 22.

9. Out from the south proceedeth the hot blast ;
   And from Mezarim [1] comes the biting cold.
10. The wind of GOD [2] produces the hoar-frost ;
    The waters, wide, are all congealed by it.
11. With rain he ladeneth the thick dark cloud,
    And dissipates the filmy cumulus [3] :
12. It turneth round about as He doth guide,
    That His commandment it may execute
    Upon the [vast] expanse of all the Earth. [4]
13. Whether in chastisement ; or for His land ;
    Or, He, in mercy, causeth it to come.

w. (page 178) chap. xxxvii. 14-22. *Application and Exhortation to consider God's wondrous works.*

14. O Job ! [I pray thee] hearken unto this ;
    Stand still and contemplate GOD's [5] wondrous works.
15. Know'st THOU how Eloah gives charge to them,
    And how He make His light on them to shine ?
16. Or dost thou know the thick-clouds' balancings,
    His wondrous works, Whose knowledge hath no bound ? [6]
17. How [is it that] thy garments [feel so] warm,
    When He makes still the Earth, with Southern heat ?
18. Did'st thou help [7] Him [when] He spread out the sky ;
    And made it like a molten mirror [firm] ? [8]

---

[1] We take מְזָרִים (*mezarim*) as synonymous with מַזָּרוֹת (*mazzaroth*) of ch. xxxviii. 32 (the former having the masc. pl. ending ; and the latter, the fem. pl.) The word denotes the signs of the Zodiac, and the reference is to the fact of cold winds being associated with the sun's position in certain Signs. Some take it from זָרָה (*zārăh*) to sc'atter ; though what sense this makes it is difficult to see.

[2] Heb., *El.*

[3] Heb., *cloud of his light* : *i.e.*, the thin bright cloud which disperses and disappears as a sign of fine weather ; in contrast with the dark gathering cloud which becomes darker and increases in size as it is laden with rain, and is therefore a sign of wet weather.

[4] See the Oxford Gesenius.

[5] Heb., *El.*

[6] Heb., *perfect of knowledges.*

[7] Heb., *with Him.*

[8] Or, *smooth.*

19. Oh, tell me¹ that which we should say to Him ;
   We know not what to say ;² so dark³ are we!
20. Must He be told that I would speak to him?
   For none can see or speak with Him, and live.⁴
21. But now, [though] men see not the light [of God]
   Yet He is bright [in splendour ⁵] in the skies :
   But when the wind has passed and cleared the clouds,
22-. Then, from the North, there comes a golden light.⁶

G. (page 178) xxxvii. 23, 24.   *Conclusion.   On God's behalf.*

-22. Ah ! with Eloah there is majesty
23. Divine.⁷   And Shaddai : we cannot find
   Him out : so great is He in pow'r ; so full
   Of righteousness, and truth : He'll not afflict.
24. Therefore, can men, but stand in awe of Him :
   For none can know Him, though they're wise of heart.⁸

---

¹ One school of Massorites has the first person plural, as in the Text. Receptus. The other school has the first person singular (" me ") written, and " us " read. But some codices (with Sept. and Syr.) have " me " both written and read. See Ginsburg's Heb. Text and note.

² Heb., *we cannot arrange our words.*

³ Heb., *by reason of darkness*, which is put by *Metonymy* for ignorance.

⁴ See Exod. xix. 21 ; xxxiii. 20. and compare Gen. xxxii. 30. Judg. vi. 22 ; xiii. 22.

⁵ Heb., בָּהִיר *(bāhīr)* only here. From the same root we have

בַּהֶרֶת *(bahereth) a bright spot* Lev. xiii. 2, &c., bright, and burning, and shining.

⁶ Heb., *gold.* The meaning is that man by nature is utterly ignorant. He knows nothing of God in heaven above. All is darkness there to him. Yet God is there in all His wondrous glory. And just as when a storm has dispersed all the dark clouds and cleared the air, so, when God reveals Himself, His light and truth are seen.

⁷ Heb., *awful* or *terrible*, but only because Divine.

⁸ Heb., *not all (i.e.,* not any of) *the wise in heart can see Him :* " See being put by *Metonymy* for *know.*

JEHOVAH AND JOB

D. (page 54) chaps. xxxviii. 1—xlii. 6.

D ┌ A │ a │ xxxviii. 1—xl. 2.   Jehovah's first address.
   │   │   b │ xl. 3-5.   Job's first answer.
   │
   │ *A* │ *a* │ xl. 6—xli. 34.   Jehovah's second address.
   └   │   *b* │ xlii. 1-6.   Job's second answer.

---

a. (above) chap. xxxviii.—xl. 2.   *Jehovah's first address.*

a │ B¹ │ xxxviii. 1-3.   Jehovah's *first* appeal to Job.
   │   C¹ │ xxxviii. 4-35.   The Inanimate Creation. Wisdom exhibited in outward activities.
   │   B² │ xxxviii. 36-38.   Jehovah's *second* appeal to Job.
   │   C² │ 39—xxxix. 30.   The Animate Creation. Wisdom manifested "in the inward parts."
   │   B³ │ xl. 1, 2.   Jehovah's *third* appeal to Job.

B ¹. (page 185) chap. xxxviii. 1-3. *Jehovah's first appeal.*

1. Then Jehovah spake¹ to Job out of the storm,² and said :
2. Who is he who thus maketh counsel dark
   By words devoid of knowledge [and of truth] ?
3. Gird up thy loins now, like a man ;³ for I
   Will ask of thee, and thou shalt answer Me.

C ¹. (page 185) chap. xxxviii. 4-35. *The Inanimate Creation.*
     (*Wisdom exhibited in outward activities.*)

C ¹ | D | 4-7. The Earth.

    E | c ¹ | 8-11. The Sea. ⎫ Things
        d | 12-15. The Morn, and Dawn. ⎬ pertaining
        c ² | 16-18. The Springs of the Sea. ⎭ to the Earth.

        F | 19-.   Light. ⎫ Things pertaining to
                     ⎬ both the Earth
        F | -19-21. Darkness. ⎭ and the Heavens.

    E | *c* ¹ | 22, 23. Snow and Hail. ⎫ Things
         d | 24-27. Lightning. ⎬ pertaining to
         c ² | 28-30. Rain, Dew and Frost. ⎭ the Heavens.

   D | 31-35. The Heavens.

---

¹ See chap. iv. 1 note.

² Heb., *Storm* or *tempest ;* not " whirlwind. See Ps. cvii. 25 ; cxlviii. 4. Ezek. i. 4 ; xiii. 11, 13 ; and perhaps Is. xxix. 6. Doubtless, it refers to the storm which Elihu seems to see approaching (ch. xxxvii. 15-24.) The article refers to something known or already intimated to the reader.

³ Heb., גֶּבֶר (*gever*) *a strong man.* See note on ch. iv. 17.

D. (page 186) chap. xxxviii. 4-7. *The Earth.*

4. Where wast thou when I Earth's foundations laid ?
   Say, if thou know and understandest [1] it.
5. Who fix'd its measurements (for thou wilt know [2]) ?
   Or, Who upon it stretchèd out the line ?
6. On what were its foundations made to rest ?
   Or, Who, its corner-stone [so truly] laid ;
7. (When all the morning stars in chorus sang,
   And all the sons of God [3] did shout for joy) [4] ?

c [1]. (page 186) chap. xxxviii. 8-11. *The Sea.*

8. Or, Who fenced in with doors the [roaring] Sea,
   When bursting forth from [Nature's] womb it came ?
9. What time I made the clouds its covering-robe,
   And darkness deep, the swaddling-band thereof ;
10. When I decreed for it My boundary,
    And set its bars and doors, and to it said,
11.   'Thus far—no farther, Ocean, shalt thou come :
      'Here shalt thou [5] stay the swelling of thy waves ?'

The phrase דַּעַת בִּינָה (*daath bīnah*) is too intensive for the tame rendering of the A.V. Its only other occurrence is in Prov. iv. 1. It means *to know understanding*. Now in Prov. iv. 5 is the express warning "Lean not on thine own understanding" (See too Prov. xxiii. 4) : *i.e.:* lean not on it for support. Our own understanding thus stands in opposition to true understanding which must needs be Divinely taught.

[2] Or, if thou knowest what understanding is ! which no man knows.

[3] *i.e., the angels;* as always in the Old Test. See note on chap. i. 6.

[4] Compare Ezra iii. 10-13. Neh. xii. 27, which custom is probably traced back to this Scripture.

[5] "*Thou.*" So it should be, with Aramaic, Syriac and Vulgate versions. See Ginsburg's Text and note.

d. (page 186) chap. XXXVIII. 12-15.   *The Morn and Dawn*

12. Hast thou called Morning forth [1] since thou wast born ; [2]
  Or taught the early Dawn to know its place ;
13. [Bid Morn] lay hold on outskirts of the Earth,
  [Taught Dawn] to rout [3] the lawless from their place ?
14. [Bid Morn] change Earth [4] as clay beneath the seal ;
  [Bid Dawn] enrobe the beauteous world [5] with light ?
15. Thus Morning robs the wicked of their prey, [6]
  And stays, arrested, the uplifted arm.

c [2]. (page 186) chap. XXXVIII. 16-18.   *The Springs of the Sea.*

16. The fountains of the Sea : Hast thou explored ?
  Or, Hast thou searched the secrets of the Deep ?
17. The gates of Death : Have they been shown to thee ?
  Or, Hast thou seen the portals of its shade ?
18. The utmost breadths of Earth : Hast thou surveyed ?
  Reply, if thou hast knowledge of it all.

---

[1] The verbs in verses 13-15 are all in the Future ; and all (with one exception) precede, instead of following, their Nominative. Hence, they would seem to be in the nature of Passives, depending on the "*bidden*" and "*taught*" which have gone before ; or upon the word "*saying*," understood. The Structure in that case would be a repeated alternation—

  v [1] | 12-. Bidden morn since thy birth.

   w [1] | -12. Taught Dawn to know its place.

  v [2] | 13-. Bidden Morn to lay hold of Earth's outskirts.

   w [2] | -13. Taught Dawn to say to the wicked 'Be routed out.'

  v [3] | 14-. Bidden Morn to transform the earth.

   w [3] | -14. Bid Dawn to clothe all in beauty.

[2] Heb., *since thy days ; i.e.,* from thy first days, or earliest day.

[3] Heb., *to be shaken out* like crumbs from a cloth.

[4] Heb., *She : i.e.,* the earth.

[5] Heb., *They : i.e.,* the outskirts of the earth ; or, all things.

[6] Or, *deprives the wicked of their day.* Lit., *From the wicked, their light is witholden : i.e.,* the night (which is *their* day) is ended by the Dawn. Compare chap. xxiv. 13-16. What is actually meant is expressed in our rendering "robs the wicked of their prey," for the two lines are synthetic.

F. and *F.* (page 186) chap. xxxviii. 19-21. *Light **and** Darkness.*

19. Where lies the way that leads to Light's abode ?
    And as for Darkness : Where's the place thereof,
20. That thou shouldst bring each to its proper bound,
    And know the paths that lead unto its house ?
21. Thou know'st [of course] : thou must have been then **born** ;
    And great must be the number of thy days !

c [1]. (page 186) chap. xxxviii. 22, 23. *Snow and Hail.*

22. The treasuries of Snow : Hast thou approach'd ?
    Or, Hast thou seen the store-house of the Hail,
23. Which 'gainst a time of trouble I have kept,
    Against the day of battle and of war ? [1]

d [2]. (page 186) chap. xxxviii. 24-27. *Lightning and Thunder.*

24. By what way part themselves the rays of Light ?
    How drives the East-wind o'er the earth its course ?
25. Who cleft a channel for the floods of rain ?
    Or passage for the sudden thunder-flash ;
26. So that it rains on lands where no one dwells ;
    On wilderness where no man hath his home ;
27. To saturate the wild and thirsty waste ;
    And cause the meadows' tender herb to shoot ?

c [2]. (page 186) xxxviii. 28-30. *Rain, Dew, and Frost.*

28. The Rain : hath it a father [besides Me] ?
    The drops of dew : Who hath begotten them ?
29. Whose is the womb whence cometh forth the Ice ?
    And heaven's hoar-frost : Who gave to it its birth ?

---

[1] Compare Jos. x. 11. Isa. xxx. 30. Ezek. xiii. 11, 13; and specially Rev. xvi. 21.

30. As, turned to stone, the waters hide themselves,
   The surface of the deep, congeal'd, coheres,[1]

D. (page 186) chap. xxxviii. 31–35.   *The Heavens.*

31. Canst thou bind fast the cluster Pleiades ?
   Or, Canst thou loosen [great] Orion's bands ?
32. Canst thou lead forth the Zodiac's [2] monthly Signs ?
   Or, Canst thou guide Arcturus [3] and his sons ?
33. The statutes of the heavens : know'st thou these ?
   Didst thou set its [4] dominion o'er the earth ?
34. The clouds: to them canst thou lift up thy voice,
   That plenteousness of rain may cover thee ?
35. Canst thou send lightings forth, that they may go
   And say to thee ' Behold us ! Here are we ! '

B[2]. (page 185) chap. xxxviii. 36-38.   *Jehovah's Second appeal
   to Job.*

36. Who hath put wisdom in the inward parts ?
   Or, understanding given to the heart ?
37. Who, by his wisdom piles the clouds in tiers ?
   Or, Who inclines [5] the rain-clouds of the skies ?[6]
38. When dust, like metal fused,[7] becometh hard,
   And clods cleave fast together solidly.[8]

---

[1] Heb., *take or catch hold of each* ***other :*** *i.e.*, cohere when frozen. **See** ch. xli. 17.

[2] Heb., *Mazzaroth*, or the twelve **signs** of the Zodiac.

[3] Arcturus : *i.e.*, the Polar Star **and** Constellations.

[4] Heb., *his : i.e.*, the heaven, and **its** dominion over the earth.

[5] Heb., *to cause to lie down* ; **hence,** *to incline* a vessel so as to **empty** it.

[6] Heb., *bottles of the skies.*

[7] Heb., מוּצָק (*mûtzach*) *fused*, solid **metal.** *i.e.*, when the rain clouds are

emptied out, the dust is caused first to run into a mass of mire, like molten metal ; which afterward, when the clouds are emptied, becomes a hard clod, like solid metal.

[8] These three verses form the introduction to the Animate Creation, which manifests God's " wisdom in the inward parts." These phenomena affect the earth as the home of the animals especially with respect to their food and their *sustenance*, which is first dealt with in the case of the Lion **and the** Raven.

C². (page 185) xxxviii. 36—xxxix. 30.   *The Animate Creation.*
(*Wisdom manifested in the inward parts.*)

C² | G | **xxxviii. 39-41.**   Sustenance.   (The Lion, *vv.* 39, 40.
The Raven, *v.* 41.)

    H | **xxxix. 1-4.**   Young.   (The wild Goats, *v.* 1-.   The
Hinds, *vv.* -1-4.)

      I | **xxxix. 5-12.**   Attribute.   Freedom.   (The wild
Ass, *vv.* 5-8.   The wild Bull, *vv.* 9-12.)

    H | **xxxix. 13-18.**   Young.   (The Ostrich.)

      I | **xxxix. 19-25.**   Attribute.   Courage.   (The War-
horse.)

  G | **xxxix. 26-30.**   Sustenance.   (The Hawk, *v.* 26.   The
Eagle, *vv.* 27-30.)

G. (above) chap. xxxviii. 39-41.   *Sustenance.   The Lion.*

39. The Lion : wilt thou hunt for him his prey ?
    Or satisfy the young lions' appetite,
40. What time within their dens they lay them down,
    Or, in their jungle lairs they lie in wait ?

The Raven.

41. Who is it that provides the Raven meat?
    When unto GOD[1] his young ones lift their cry,
    And wander forth abroad from lack of food.

---

[1] Heb., *El.*

H. (page 191) xxxix. 1-4. *Young.* (*The wild Goats and Hinds.*)

xxxix. 1. Know'st thou the time the Rock-Goat[1] gendereth ?
      Observest thou the calving of the Hinds ?

    2. The months they fill ? Didst thou the number set,
      And know the time when they to birth should bring ?

    3. They bow themselves : they bring their offspring forth,
      And to the winds cast all their pangs away.

    4. Strong grow their young, they fatten on the plains ;
      And to their parents never more return.[2]

I. (page 191) xxxix. 5-12. *Attribute.* (*Freedom.*)

The Wild Ass.

    5. Who is it that sent forth the Wild-Ass free ?
      Or who hath loosened the swift-runner's[3] bands ?

    6. Whose dwelling I have made the wilderness,
      His haunts, the salt and arid desert waste.

    7. The city's busy tumult he doth scorn,
      The driver's shouts and cries[4] he doth not hear.

    8. The mountains are his ample pasture ground ;
      There roameth he in quest of all things green.

The Wild Bull.

    9. The Wild Bull : Will he be thy willing slave,
      Or pass the night, contented, by thy crib ?

---

[1] *i.e.*, the wild he-goats. In ch. xxi. 10 the first line speaks of the gendering of the *bull*, and the second speaks of the calving of the *cow*. Moreover, יָלַד (*yālad*) means *to beget* (in Kal), as well as *to bring forth*. See Gen. iv. 18, where it is used of a man : "Irad *begat* Mehujael."

[2] Heb., *they go forth, and return not to them : i.e.*, to their parents.

[3] It is the same animal in both lines, though with different names : The two names, in the East, to-day, are thus used : the first of *the swift runner* ; and the second *the fleeing one* or *fugitive.*

[4] Heb., *noises*—made up of shouts and cries.

10. To plough, Canst thou in harness lead him forth ?
    To harrow, Will he follow after thee ?
11. Wilt thou, for all his strength, confide in him ?
    Or, leave to him the tillage of thy ground ?
12. Canst thou be sure he will bring home thy seed,
    Or gather corn to fill thy threshing-floor.

H. (page 191) xxxix. 13-18. *Young.* *The Ostrich.*

13. The Ostrich wing, admirèd tho' it be ;
    Is it the pinion of the kindly Stork ?
14. Nay ! she it is that leaves to earth her eggs,
    And in the dust she letteth them be warmed,
15. Unmindful that the passing foot might crush,
    Or that the roaming beast might trample them.
16. She dealeth sternly with her young, as if
    Not hers : and fears not that her toil be vain.
17. For, God created her devoid of sense ;
    Nor gave her in intelligence a share.
18. What time she lifteth up herself for flight
    The horse and rider both alike she scorns.

I. (page 191) chap. xxxix. 19-25. *Attribute.* (*Courage.*)
The War-horse.

19. The War-horse : Didst thou give to him his strength ?
    Or clothe his arching neck with quivering mane ?
20. Made him leap lightly as the locust does ?
    The glory of his snorting fills with dread.
21. He paws the plain, rejoicing in his strength :
    He rusheth on to meet the armèd host.
22. He mocks at fear and cannot be dismayed ;
    Nor from the sword will he turn back or flee.
23. Though 'gainst him rain the arrows of the foe,
    The glitter of the lance, and flash of spear.

24. With noise and fury stampeth [1] he the earth :
    Nor standeth steady when the trumpet sounds.
25. And when it sounds amain[2] he saith, Ahah !
    And scents the coming battle from afar,
26. The captain's thunder,[3] and the shouts [4] of war.

G. (page 191) chap. xxxix. 26-30. *Sustenance.*

The Hawk.

26. Is it by thine instruction that the Hawk
    Soars high ; and spreads his pinions [5] to the South ?

The Eagle.

27. It is at thy command the Eagle mounts,
    And builds his eyrie in the lofty heights ?
28. The rock he makes his home ; and there he dwells
    On crag's sharp tooth and [lonely] fastnesses.
29. And thence he keenly spieth out the prey ;
    His piercing eye beholds it from afar.
30. His young one's learn full soon to suck up blood
    And where the slain are lying, there is he.[6]

B [3]. (page 185) chap. xl. 1, 2. *Jehovah's third appeal to Job.*

xl. 1. And Jehovah appealed[7] to Job from out the storm, and
    said :
   2. As caviller [8] with [mighty] Shaddai,
      Contender with Eloah ; answer that !

---

[1] Heb., *they paw.* But *he diggeth* according to Sept., Syr., and Vulg. See Ginsburg's Text and note.

[2] Heb., *in abundance of trumpet.*

[3] *i.e.,* the stentorian shouts.

[4] Heb., *shouting.*

[5] So *read ;* but *written* " wing " (sing.). In some Codices, with two early printed editions, it is both read and written plural : " wings." See Ginsburg's Text and note.

[6] Compare Matt. xxiv. 28.

[7] " Answered and said " is an *Idiom,* and the word " answered" must be rendered in accordance with whatever is said : *e.g.,* Prayed and said; asked and said. Here Jehovah concluded his first address by this appeal. See note on ch. iv. 1.

[8] Gesenius has clearly shown that this is not a verb, but a noun.

b. (page 185) chap. xl. 3-5.   *Job's first answer.*

3. And Job replied, and said :—
4. Lo! I am vile! What shall I answer Thee?
   Rather, I lay my hand upon my mouth.
5. Already, I have spoken far too much; [1]
   I cannot answer.   I [2] will add no more.

---

a. (page 185) xl. 6—xli. 34.   *Jehovah's second Address.*

a | J [1] | xl. 6-13. Jehovah's first appeal to Divine power. (General.)

K[1] | xl. 14.   Consequent admission.

J [2] | xl. 15.—xli. 10-. Jehovah's second appeal to Divine power.
(Special.) Behemoth (xl. 15-24). Leviathan (xli. 1-10-).

K[2] | xli. -10, 11.   Consequent inference.

J [3] | xli. 12-34.   Jehovah's third appeal to Divine power.
(Special.) Leviathan, continued.

---

[1] Heb., *Once I have spoken, but I will not proceed.*
Yea, twice, but I will add no more. "Once, twice," being the Heb. Idiom for *repeatedly,* we have rendered it as above.

[2] We omit the word "but" with some codices, and Sept. and Vulg. versions. See Ginsburg's Text and note.

J [1]. (page 195) chap. **xl.** 6-13. *Appeal to his power.* (*General.*)

xl. 6. Then Jehovah again addressed[1] Job out of the **storm,**
   and said :
   7. Now, like a strong man gird thou up thy loins :
   'Tis I who ask thee; make thou Me to know.
   8. Wilt thou MY righteousness quite disannul ?
   And ME condemn, that thou may righteous seem ?
   9. Hast thou an arm then, like the mighty GOD ? [2]
   Or, Can'st thou thunder with a voice like His ?
   10. Deck thyself now with glory and with might :
   Array thyself with majesty and power.
   11. Send far and wide thy overflowing wrath :
   And on each proud one look, and bring him low ;
   12. Each proud one single out, and humble him ;
   Yea, crush the evil-doers where they stand.
   13. Hide them away together in the dust ;
   Their persons in the deepest dungeon bind.

K [1]. (page 195) chap. **xl.** 14. *Consequent admission.*

   14. THEN, ALSO, I MYSELF WILL OWN TO THEE
   THAT THY RIGHT HAND, TO SAVE THEE,
   WILL SUFFICE.

J [2] . (page 195) chaps. **xl.** 15—xli. 10-. *Appeal to Divine Power.*
   (*Special.*)

(*Behemoth.*) [3]

   15. Behold Behèmoth now, which I have made
   As well as thee : grass like the Ox he eats.

---

[1] See note, above, on ch. xl. 1.

[2] Heb., *El.*

[3] The Structure of this member concerning Behemoth (ch. xl. 15-29) seems to be as follows :—

x	15.	Behemoth and his food.
y	16-18.	Man unable to resist his strength.
y	19.	God, his Maker, alone able to deal with him.
x	20-24.	Behemoth : his haunts and food.

16. Behold, his massive strength is in his loins :
    His force doth in his belly's muscles lie ;
17. Shakes he his tail ? 'Tis like a cedar tree.
    The sinews of his thighs are firm entwined.
18. His bones are strong, like unto tubes of brass ;
    His ribs, with bars of iron may compare.
19. A master-piece of all God's ways is he :
    Only his Maker can bring nigh his sword.[1]
20. The mountains will bring produce forth for him,
    While all the beasts do, fearless, round him play.
21. Beneath the shady trees he lieth down,
    And rests in covert of the reed and fen.
22. The shady trees weave o'er him each its shade ;
    While willows of the brook encompass him.
23. Suppose the stream should swell ; he will not blench :
    Unmoved, tho' swollen Jordan reach his mouth.
24. Shall any take him while he lies on watch ?
    Or, with a hook shall any pierce his nose ?

(Leviathan.)

xli. 1. Canst thou draw up Leviathan with hook ?
    Or catch as with [an angler's] line, his tongue ?
2. Canst thou insert into his nose, a reed ?
    Or, Canst thou pierce his jaw through with a thorn ?
3. Will he make many humble pray'rs to thee ?
    Or, Will he ever say soft things to thee ?
4. Will he engage in covenant with thee
    That thou should'st take him for thy life-long slave ?[2]
5. Wilt thou, as with some linnet, play with him ?
    Or, Wilt thou cage him for thy maidens' sport ?
6. Will trading dealers haggle o'er his price ?
    And retail[3] him among the merchantmen ?

---

[1] *i.e.*, the sword that is able to slay Behemoth.
[2] Heb., *servant of olām ; i.e., a* servant *for ever.* See Ex. xxi. 6. Deut. xv. 17.
[3] Heb., *divide* or *parcel out.*

   7. Wilt thou with darts attempt to fill his skin?
      Or [fill] his head with spears for catching fish?[1]
   8. Lay thou thy hand upon him, though but once;
      Think only of the contest, do no more.
   9. Behold, all hope of taking him is vain:
      Ev'n at the sight of him one is cast down.
10-. None so fool-hardy as to stir him up.

K[2] (page 195) chap. xli. -10, 11. *Consequent Inference.*

-10. BEFORE ME, THEN, [HIS MAKER] WHO CAN
     STAND?
 11. WHO E'ER FIRST GAVE TO ME, THAT I SHOULD
     HIM
     REPAY? SINCE ALL BENEATH THE HEAV'NS
     IS MINE?

J[3] (page 195) chap. xli. 12-34. *Appeal to Divine Power.*
(Special.)

Leviathan (continued).

12. About his parts, silence, I must not keep:
    His wondrous strength; his well-proportioned frame.
13. His coat of mail: Who hath e'er stripped this off?
    His double row of teeth: Who enters there?
14. The doors which close his mouth[2]: who opens them?
    His teeth's surroundings are a scare to see.
15. The scales which form his armour are his pride,
    Each one shut up and closed as with a seal.
16. So near, one to another do they lie,
    That air, between them, cannot find a way:
17. So close unto each other do they cleave,
    And cleave so fast that none can sunder them.

---

[1] Heb., *spear of fishes : i.e.,* spears made for catching fish.
[2] Heb., *face.*

18. His sneezings are a flashing forth of light ;
    His eyes are like the eye-lids of the Dawn.
19. Out of his mouth, vapours like torches go,
    And sparks like fire, therefrom, make their escape.
20. Out of his nostrils goeth forth a smoke,
    As from a boiling pot on reed-fire set.
21. His breath,—as if it would set coals on fire,
    And from his mouth a flame seems issuing forth.
22. His strength abideth ever in his neck ;
    Before his face grim terror, fleeing, goes.[1]
23. His softer folds of flesh, though hanging, cleave
    So close on him that moved they cannot be.
24. His heart is hard, e'en like unto a stone ;
    Aye, like a nether millstone firm and hard.
25. Whene'er he riseth up, the mighty fear :
    And at the waves he makes,[2] their terror's great.
26. Let one encounter him—no sword will stand :
    Nor spear, nor dart, nor iron coat-of-mail.
27. Iron he counts no better than a straw,
    And brass, no better is than rotten wood.[3]
28. The arrow [4] will not make him flee away :
    Sling-stones are only stubble unto him.
29. Like harmless chaff he counts the pond'rous club ;
    And, at the whizzing of a spear, will laugh.
30. His under-parts are sharply-pointed spikes ;
    He spreads like threshing-drag upon the mire.
31. Like boiling pot he makes the deep to foam :
    And like a well-stirred ointment pot, the Nile.
32. His wake he makes a sparkling, shiny path :
    So that the deep will look like hoary hair.

---

[1] *i.e.*, the terror which his approach excites is personified and represented as dancing in advance of him. The line might thus fairly be rendered :—" Before him people flee, with terror struck."

[2] Heb., *by the reason of the breakers : i.e.*, the breakers on the shores caused by the waves created by his rising from the waters.

[3] Heb., *wood of rottenness.*

[4] Heb., *son of the bow.*

33. His equal is not found, on all the earth.
    He hath been made insensible of fear.
34. On all things high he looketh [dauntlessly] ;
    And, over all proud beasts,[1] himself is king.

      b. (page 185) xlii. 1-6. *Job's second answer.*

xlii. 1. Then Job answered Jehovah and said :—
    2. I know, I know, that THOU can'st all things do.
      No purposes of THINE can be withstood.
    3. [Thou askedst][2]
               'Who is this that counsel hides
            'And darkens all, because of knowledge void?'
      'Tis I ! I uttered things I could not know ;
      Things far too wonderful, and past my ken.
    4. But hear, I pray thee : let me speak this once.
      [Thou said'st][3]
             'Tis I who ask thee : Answer Me.'
    5. I'd heard of Thee with hearing of the ear,
      But now that I[4] have had a sight of Thee
    6. Wherefore, I loathe myself ; and I repent
      In dust and ashes.

---

[1] Heb., *all the sons of pride ;* idiom for *all proud* beasts.
[2] Chap. xxxviii. 2.
[3] Chap. xxxviii. 3 and xl. 7.
[4] Heb., *mine eye*, put, by *Synecdoche*, for *myself.*

THE THREE FRIENDS: THEIR DEPARTURE

C. (page 54) xlii. 7-9.

C | A | 7-. Jehovah ceases to speak to Job.

    B | -7-. Jehovah speaks to Job's Friends.

        C | a | -7-. What He said.

            b | -7. The reason : " because."

        C | *a* | 8-. What they were to do.

            b | -8-. The reason : " because."

    B | 9-. Job's Friends obey Jehovah.

  A | -9. Jehovah accepts Job.

A | 7-. And it came to pass after Jehovah had spoken these words [ch. xxxviii.—xli.] unto Job

    B | -7. that Jehovah [spoke] to Eliphaz the Temanite, and said:

        C | a | -7-. My wrath is kindled against thee, and against thy two friends :

            b | -7. because ye have not spoken of[1] me the thing which is right[2] as My servant Job hath.[3]

        C | *a* | 8-. Now therefore take unto you seven bullocks and seven rams, and go unto My servant Job, and offer up for yourselves a burnt offering : and My servant Job shall pray for you ; (for him[4] will I accept),[4] that I deal not with you after your folly.

            b | -8. because ye have not spoken of[1] Me the thing which is right[2] as My servant Job hath.[3]

    B | 9-. So Eliphaz the Temanite and Bildad the Shuite [and][5] Zophar the Naamathite went and did according to that which Jehovah had commanded them.

A | -9. And Jehovah accepted Job.[4]

For notes 1—5 see next page.

SATAN'S DEFEAT: JOB BLESSED WITH DOUBLE

B. (page 54) chap. xlii. 10-13.

B | D | 10. Job's blessing.
        E | 11. His family.
    D | 12. Job's blessing.
        E | 13. His family.

D | 10-. And Jehovah himself turned the captivity ⁶ of Job, when he had prayed for his friends : ⁷ and Jehovah increased all that Job had possessed, two-fold.

   E | 11. Then came there unto him, all his brethren, and all his sisters, and all his former acquaintances,⁸ and they did eat bread with him in his house : and shewed sympathy with him,⁹ and comforted him for all the calamity which Jehovah had brought upon him : and each one gave him a sum ¹⁰ of money and each one [gave him] a ring of gold.

D | 12. So Jehovah blessed the latter end of Job more than his beginning : ¹¹ and he had 14,000 sheep, and 6,000 camels, and 1,000 yoke of oxen, and 1,000 she-asses.

   E | 13. He had also seven sons, and three daughters.

---

¹ Heb., אֶל (*el*) to or unto. It is the sign of the dative case. It may mean *concerning*; but this is not its primary meaning.

² Or, *the right thing.*

³ The right thing that Job had spoken is recorded in ch. xlii. 1-6. This is what Jehovah here refers to. All was more or less wrong before. This was the manifestation of true "wisdom": that wisdom which is Divine, and cometh down from above. See note on ch. xxviii. 28. Also comments on it in Part I. *The oldest lesson in the world.* The three friends had not (yet) said this right thing.

⁴ Heb., *his face*: put by Synecdoche for the whole person.

⁵ Some Codices, with Syriac and Vulg. have this "and." See Ginsburg's Text and note.

⁶ A Heb. *Idiom* for causing trouble to pass away.

⁷ Heb., *for his friend*: *i.e.*, for each of them.

⁸ Heb., *all his knowers*: *i.e.*, all who had known him before his troubles.

⁹ Heb., *shook their heads with him.*

¹⁰ Heb., *Kesita*, as in Gen. xxxiii. 19. *One* piece or *one* sum.

¹¹ This blessing also was included in "the end of the Lord" (Jas. v. 17).

CONCLUSION

A. (page 54) chap. xlii. 14-17.

(End of his family history.)

```
A  | F | 13-15.  Job's children.
   |    G | 16-.  His age.
   | F | -16.  Job's grandchildren.
   |    G | -16.  His death.
```

F | 13-15. And the one they called [1] Jemima,[2] and the second they called Kezia,[3] and the third they called Keren-happuch.[4] And in all the land there were no women found so beautiful[5] as the daughters of Job: and their father gave them an inheritance among [6] their brethren.

   G | 16-. And Job lived after this a hundred and forty years.[7]

F | -16. And saw his sons, and his sons' sons, even four generations.

   G | 17. So Job died, old and full of days.

---

[1] The Heb., וַיִּקְרָא (*vay-yikrah*) is indefinite. It does not follow, therefore, that Job so named them. They are rather appellations bestowed on them by the people on account of their beauty.

[2] *i.e.*, possibly *dove-eyed*, comp. Cant. i. 15 ; ii. 14 ; iv. 1. Or *fair as the day*.

[3] Heb., *cassia : i.e.*, sweet as the essence of cassia.

[4] Heb., *paint-box :* as though needing no artificial painting like others (see 2 Kings ix. 30 ; Jer. iv. 30 ; Ezek. xxiii. 40). She was in herself so beautiful that she did not require to be painted like others.

[5] Heb., *fair*. But we use the word rather of complexion than of appearance. Our English idiom is "beautiful."

[6] Compare Num. xxvii. 4-8; xxxvi. 8 ; Josh. xv. 18, 19.

[7] This probably (though not necessarily), means after his calamities. If his double blessing includes years his age before might have been the half, *i.e.*, 70 years, and the whole 210 years. The Sept. adds here " and all the days of Job were 240 years." See Ginsburg's Text and note.